Ferruccio Canali

MANTUA

HISTORY AND ART

254 illustrations
5 itineraries

photographs:
Giovanni Rodella

BET
BONECHI EDIZIONI "IL TURISMO" FIRENZE

The Publishing House would like to thank all those who have helped in realizing this work, and in particular:
Palazzo Ducale: Prof. Aldo Ciccinelli, Amos Zerbini
Palazzo Te: Prof. Ugo Bazzotti
The Diocese of Mantua:
Mons. Ciro Ferrari
D.ssa Irma Pagliari
Don Italo Zanoni
Don Rino Garosi
Don Luigi Grossi
Don Renato Pavese
Primo Mattioli
Antonio Lodigiani
Geom. Ippolito Cazzaniga Danesmondi
Tecnolumen-Castel Goffredo

Photos: Archives of Bonechi Edizioni "Il Turismo" S.r.l. realized by Giovanni Rodella
     I-Buga Sas. Milan: pages 6-7, cover photo (Aut.SMA n.023 of 04-02-94)
Layout and cover: Lorenzo Cerrina
English translation: Erika Pauli for Studio Comunicare
Text editor: Lorena Lazzari
Photolithography: La Fotolitografia, Florence
Printed: BO.BA.DO.MA., Florence
ISBN 88-7204-294-1

HISTORICAL NOTES

The founding of the city of Mantua, both legendary and historical, still remains somewhat of a mystery. Mythological sources as well as tales of the founding heroes differ, although various passages in the oldest stories may coincide with reality. Mantua was probably founded by the Etruscans, who had occupied a good part of the Plain of the Po, settling near Bologna and at Spina, at the mouth of the Po. In fact a rich emporium or trading center has been discovered near Spina, whose finds bear witness to the

Upon Matilda's death in 1115, the city became a free Commune. After rebelling against the attempts of the Holy Roman emperor Frederick Barbarossa to establish imperial control, it was lacerated by internal struggles between rival families for the conquest of power. In 1328, the Bonacolsi, who had become the first Lords of Mantua in 1273, were ousted by Luigi Gonzaga, who was nominated imperial vicar the following year, marking the beginning of Gonzaga domination which was to last until 1707.

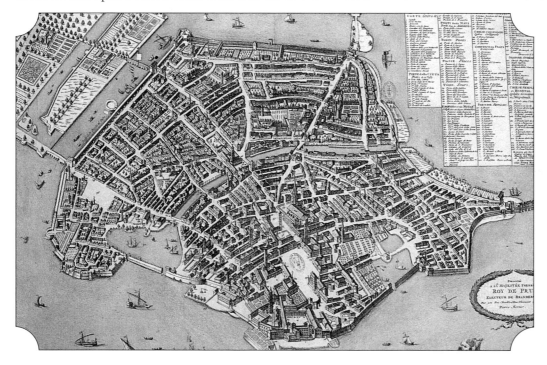

Perspective plan of the city of Mantua, after a drawing by F. B. Werner (Augsburg 1750). Note how the "Rio" (small canal) protected the historical center from possible attacks and served as the thoroughfare for trade.

fact that the nucleus of Mantua was an outpost of Etruscan expansion in the Plain (at least on the basis of trade wares of various provenance). Subsequently the city was taken by the Gauls. After the victory of Casteggio, it fell under Roman rule. The famous poet Virgil was born near present-day Pietole, a few kilometers from Mantua, and he was always proud of his origins, even when deprived of his lands and exiled to Rome after the battle of Philippi in 42 B.C. Virgil was the first to mention the founding of the city in his *Bucolics* where he narrates the drama of the peasants of this land. Bianore, son of Tiber and the nymph Manto, or Aucno (sometimes identified with Bianore), an Etruscan hero founder of Bologna, and also a son of Manto, is said to have created the first settlement here, naming it Mantua after his mother. In Dante's *Inferno*, the city is founded by the seer Manto. Invaded by the Barbarians in the third century, Mantua fell under Lombard rule in the eighth century and then passed to Matilda of Canossa.

In 1432 Gianfrancesco Gonzaga was created marchese of Mantua by the Emperor, and in 1530 Federico II was made duke. Between 1444 and 1478, with Ludovico II, the city became one of the most flourishing centers of Renaissance culture, thanks also to the presence in Mantua of Leon Battista Alberti. With Isabella d'Este, marchesa from 1490 to 1539, Gonzaga patronage reached its zenith, with the presence in the city first of Andrea Mantegna (1431-1506) and then the arrival in 1524 of Giulio Romano (Giulio Pippi known as Romano: 1492/99-1546). Under Duke Guglielmo (1550-1587), for whom the architect Giovan Battista Bertani (1516-1576) worked, and under Duke Vincenzo (1587-1612), the duchy touched the zenith of its artistic achievements, and the Ducal Palace became none other than a truly autonomous body, introverted and closed in on itself without a facade towards the city. The storming and sack of the city by Imperial troops in 1630, in a war which involved problems of dynastic succession and

strife between France and Spain, was one of the city's darkest moments. As early as 1627-28 the dukes had already begun to alienate the old art collections, selling part to the king of England. Much of what remained was carried off as plunder, and today the fine works of art commissioned by the Gonzaga are to be found scattered in all the museums of the world. Finally in 1701, when the Gonzaga-Nevers branch died out, the Emperor "of Austria" ousted the last duke, who once more denuded the Palace of all its precious furnishings. Mantua then fell to the Austrians, who turned it into a city-fortress, in other words a Viennese outpost in Italian soil, the beginning of an extremely interesting phase for commissions in the city. In 1785 the city was joined to the duchy of Milan, occupied by Napoleon (1797), returned to Austria (1799-1801), to become the capital of the Napoleonic Department of Mincio from 1801 to 1815, intimately bound to the rise of imperial French culture. With the Restoration it once more fell under Hapsburg rule, and was further fortified as one of the strongholds of the famous Austrian military "quadrilateral". In 1866 Mantua was occupied by the Piedmont troops and then annexed to the Kingdom of Italy. This seems to have done more harm than good, for the citizens were not at all happy with the policies of the central government. Mantua had completely lost the key role it had had under Austrian rule, and it was only with great difficulty that the city succeeded in obtaining a railroad connection to Modena and Verona. During World War I, the city was once more declared war zone and filled with soldiers and barracks. In 1919 manifestations connected with the aggression in Rome on various Socialist deputies, including the honorable Murari from Mantua, led to a general strike in the entire province, where the Socialist Party was very strong. This strike led to the so-called "Red Days", where soldiers and armed civilians fought a real urban guerrilla warfare, with dead and wounded on both sides. The "Popolo d'Italia", soon to become the organ of the National Fascist Party, compared "the Mincio to the Neva" (the river of the Russian Bolshevists). In the past hundred years the city has found it difficult to adapt to its new role as provincial center, with an urban and cultural structure still that

Preceding page: *view of the monumental center from the Lago Inferiore.*

Left: *view of the city from the Lago Superiore.*

of an old and prestigious "capital", much too large now for the requirements of its *contado* alone. The petrol-chemical plant installed on the east, with the Laghi in the background, was a disaster as far as development and real upgrading of the city was concerned. Instead of providing a new role for the city, located in one of the most productive agricultural areas of Europe, the plant polluted and ruined the lovely natural panoramas of the marshes of the Mincio.

Left:
Piazza Sordello.

Pages 6-7:
Bird's-eye view of the architectural complex of the Ducal Palace (it ranks third in Europe both for size and number of rooms, after the Louvre and the Vatican) with 513 rooms, 13 courtyards, squares or gardens, three of which are hanging.

ITINERARY 1: DUCAL PALACE

- Corte Vecchia (Old Court)
- Scalone delle Duchesse
- Sala di Sant'Alberto
- Corridoio del Passerino
- Appartamento della Guastalla
- Appartamento Verde
- Hanging Garden
- Appartamento dell'Imperatrice
- Appartamento dei duchi Guglielmo
  e Vincenzo
- Cortile d'Onore (Courtyard)
- Sala dei Falconi
- Saletta dei Mori
- Galleria degli Specchi
  (Hall of Mirrors)
- Salone degli Arcieri
  (Room of the Bowmen)
- Sala di Giuditta
- Sala del Labirinto
- Sala del Crogiuolo
- Room of Cupid and Psyche
- Domus Nova (or Apartment of
  Eleonora dei Medici) and the
  Pavilion Garden
- Corridoio del Bertani or of
  St. Barbara
- Apartment of the Dwarfs or
  Scala Santa
- Corte Nuova
- Appartamento della Metamorfosi or
  Galleria del Passerino
- La Rustica or Summer Apartment
- Cortile della Cavallerizza
- Galleria della Mostra
- Appartamento di Troia or of
  Federico II

- Galleria dei Mesi or dei Marmi
- Sala di Troia
- Camera delle Teste or
  Gabinetto dei Cesari
- Camerino dei Falconi
- Camera dei Cavalli
- Appartamento Grande or of
  Duke Guglielmo
- Sala di Manto
- Scalone di Enea
- Castle of San Giorgio
- Courtyard of the Castle of
  St. Giorgio
- Camera degli Sposi or
  "Camera Picta"
- Apartment of Ludovico II and
  Isabella d'Este

- Gabinetti della Paleologa or
  Palazzina of Margherita Paleologa
- New Apartment of Isabella d'Este
  in "Corte Vecchia"
- Sala della Scalcheria or of
  Leonbruno
- The Studiolo
- The Grotto
- Bertani's Arch and the Prato del
  Castello (Piazza Castello)
- Palatine Basilica of Santa Barbara

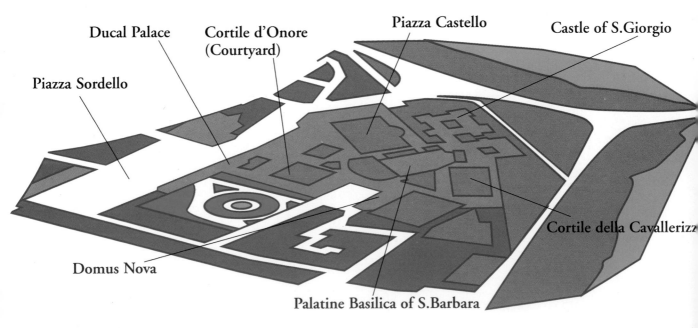

Ducal Palace

Cortile d'Onore
(Courtyard)

Piazza Castello

Castle of S.Giorgio

Piazza Sordello

Domus Nova

Cortile della Cavallerizza

Palatine Basilica of S.Barbara

PIAZZA SORDELLO

During the early middle ages, the city of Mantua was enclosed by walls which on the south coincided more or less with the buildings which embrace the

Piazza Sordello. At the center, the Cathedral, on the right, the Ducal Palace.

southern side of what is now Piazza Sordello. At the time this area was occupied by houses, streets, lanes, as well as by the much smaller Cathedral square, about as large as the space in front of the present Cathedral. In 1115, after the death of Matilda of Canossa, and the beginning of the Communal period, the City of Mantua expanded to include the rich suburbs which had grown up outside the circle of walls, and built the palaces and market squares which still characterize the town (the Piazza dell'Arengo now Broletto and the Piazza delle Erbe). When the Gonzaga Signoria gained power in 1328, the city center was once more renewed: around 1370 the vast Piazza Sordello, still there today, was created in front of the Gonzaga residence. The original route of the old Roman *cardo*, one of the two streets that crossed each other at right angles and divided the ancient settlement into quarters, probably lies along the western side of the square.

Overlooking Piazza Sordello (named after a thirteenth-century Mantuan poet, Sordello) on the north, is the Cathedral; on the east, the Magna

Domus and the Palazzo del Capitano (which can be identified by its nineteenth-century crenellations), built by the Bonacolsi and subsequently occupied by the Gonzaga as the "Corte Vecchia" of the Palazzo Ducale; on the south, the so-called Voltone di San Pietro; while on the west is the Bishop's Palace, the Palazzo degli Uberti, the Palazzo Castiglioni and, lastly, the Palazzo Acerbi.

PALAZZO DUCALE (Ducal Palace)

The complex which is generally called the Ducal Palace, or the Gonzaga Palace, consists of a series of buildings, dating to different periods, which were joined together in the course of the thirteenth to seventeenth centuries into a city within the city. This immense area of over three hectares includes fifteen enclosed open spaces (courtyards, courts, squares, gardens) and over five hundred rooms, many not open to the public. The Palace was practically abandoned in the early 1900s and some of the wings are now still semi-abandoned or in restoration

The complex vicissitudes of this Palace, with the exception of changes made in some of the rooms in

Piazza Sordello,
facade of the
Ducal Palace.

the course of centuries in line with changes in function or taste, can be summed up in the identification of a series of nuclei created *anew* or gradually "grafted on" like buds, resulting in a structure of almost labyrinthine complexity. The only way of keeping ones bearings inside during the tour or in an attempted historical reconstruction is to keep track of the historical nuclei or their transformations.

La Corte Vecchia (Old Courtyard)

The first nucleus of this vast building, located at the upper end of the *Civitas Vetus*, that is the oldest core of Mantua, belonged to the Bonacolsi family and consisted of various buildings which faced out on what was then the small Piazza della Cattedrale. These can now be identified as the Palazzo del Capitano and the *Magna Domus* on Piazza Sordello.

When the Gonzaga family rose to power in 1328, attention turned to the restructuration of the old Bonacolsi houses. The Gonzaga owned the surrounding houses and began to fuse the various lots into a single city block, closing the old lanes between buildings (a policy that was subsequently continued), so as

to create a real "Courtyard", unlike anything else in the city. Gonzaga policies from the beginning were aimed at taking over not only the levers of power, but also the physical space of the city, concretely conditioning the development and the architectural and urban structure. Around 1370 their residential complex was even furnished with enclosures of its own. The concept of the Gonzaga Palace as a city within the city thus took concrete shape, and was comprised of the so-called "Corte Vecchia", until, a few years later, around the end of the fourteenth century, Bartolino da Novara built the castle of San Giorgio to protect the lakes and serve as the Gonzaga stronghold. At the same time the old Piazza della Cattedrale was enlarged by demolishing a row of buildings which divided the area into two open spaces of equal size, thus making way for the great Piazza Sordello.

At the beginning of the fifteenth century the Gonzaga had been officially recognized as the Marchesi of the city (1432). The next step was to further enlarge the Palace by having Luca Fancelli build the nucleus of the *Domus Nova* and the wings which enclose the Cortile d'Onore, or courtyard, as well as a series of transformations inside, as in the case of the courtyard of the castle of San Giorgio.

Expulsion of the Bonacolsi by the Gonzaga, *by Domenico Morone, 1494. (note Piazza Sordello and the Cathedral before its renovation in 1756).*

Scalone delle Duchesse *(Staircase of the Duchesses)*

The tour begins in Piazza Sordello, with the entrance to the old nucleus of the Corte Vecchia. In 1777 Paolo Pozzo (1741-1803) built the monumental staircase which, from the entrance in Piazza Sordello, cut into the older stairs known as the Scalone delle Duchesse (1636), now on Piazza Lega Lombarda. The spacious flights of the Staircase of the Duchesses, a seventeenth-century addition to ennoble the entrance to the Palazzo Ducale, lead to the rooms on the upper floor which have been included in the museum tour.

Sala di Sant'Alberto *(Room of Sant'Alberto)*

After crossing the Sala dei Sette Scalini, with interesting remains of fourteenth-century fresco decorations, the so-called Sala di Sant'Alberto, where marble inscriptions are to be seen, contains the famous painting by Domenico Morone (1442-post 1517) of the *Expulsion of the Bonacolsi by the Gonzaga*, signed and dated 1494.

The painting gives us an idea of what the old facade of the Cathedral, built in late Gothic style by Iacobello and Pier Paolo Dalle Masegne, looked like before its renovation in 1756 (as it is today).

Corridoio del Passerino *(Passerino's Corridor)*

This corridor, which runs along the entire facade of the Palazzo del Capitano (over sixty meters), was inexistent until restoration of this part of the complex early in the twentieth century did away with the many intercommunicating rooms into which this wing, as all the others in the palace, was subdivided. The name refers, incorrectly, to the nickname of the last member of the Bonacolsi family. Restoration of the extensive fourteenth-century wooden ceiling also helped unify the room. Marble sculpture, coats of

Frieze of the mantelpiece with the Gonzaga coat of arms at the center, from the Palace of Revere (15th cent.).

Above:
Corridoio del Passerino.
Above, right:
Statues of the school of Mantegna (16th cent.).
Right:
Seated Virgil *(13th cent.)*
Far right:
Bust *of Francesco Gonzaga.*
Below:
Sleeping Cupid.

Appartamento della Guastalla
(Apartment of Guastalla)

Off the corridor is the apartment which takes its name from Anna Isabella della Guastalla, wife of the last duke of Mantua. She lived here between 1671 and 1703. The rooms date back to the medieval period but were frequently refurnished up to the eighteenth century. The wooden ceilings are part of the late sixteenth- and early seventeenth-century renovation by the architect Antonio Maria Viani, while the collections housed here include various outstanding terra-cotta works, such as the five Renaissance statues attributed to the school of Mantegna and the bust of *Francesco Gonzaga* by Giancristoforo Romano. To be noted are a series of marble statues including a *Sleeping Cupid*, the tomb effigy of *Margherita Malatesta* dating to the early 1400s by the workshop of the Dalle Masegne and the relief of *Philoctetes* attributed to Tullio Lombardo (late fifteenth century). Also of particular note is a small triptych in bone and wood from the workshop of degli Embriachi dating to the first half of the fifteenth century.

The Sala delle Imprese (Room of the Devices) contains interesting frescoes dating to the fourteenth century, including in particular a *Crucifixion* and above all a *Virgin and Child.*

arms and inscriptions are set along the walls, while above are interesting late Gothic geometric decorations; to be noted is the statue of the *seated Virgil*, dating to the 1200s and originally located on the neighboring Palazzo del Podestà (now replaced there by a copy). The fine mantelpiece, Albertian in style, comes from the Gonzaga Palazzo di Revere and is attributed to artists in the circle of Fancelli.

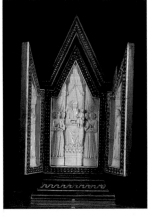

The Sala delle Sinopie contains the sinopias (preparatory drawings) found beneath Pisanello's fresco cycle in the Sala del Pisanello. It was not until 1969, after removal of the overlying early eighteenth-century decorations and restoration, that they could once more be seen.

The Sala del Pisanello (1395-*post* 1450) is a room that seems originally to have belonged to an adjacent building and was not part of the residential complex of the Dukes. The frescoes on the walls of the Arthurian legend were never completed. The artist is one of the greatest representatives of Italian International Gothic although he was also aware of the Florentine experiments with space. These scenes - painted in a mixed technique of fresco, tempera and paste with applications in gold and silver - were inspired by the deeds of the Knights of the Round Table and the Breton cycle, to which the French names written next to the various personages bear witness. Courtly ideals encountered great favor in the fifteenth-century humanist courts. To be noted in particular is the scene of the *Tournament of Louverzep*, with elegant ladies watching a lively jousting tournament from their box. The cycle may have been painted for Gianfrancesco Gonzaga, who died in 1444, but critics are still not in agreement

Left, above: Tomb effigy *of Margherita Malatesta.* Below, left to right: Virgin and Child *(14th cent.) and wooden triptych from* *the workshop of the Embriachi.*

Right, above and below*: Sinopias by Pisanello. Scenes from the* Tournament of Louverzep.

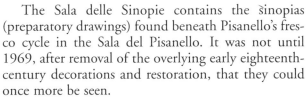

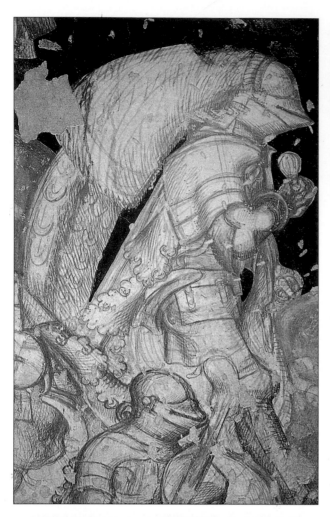

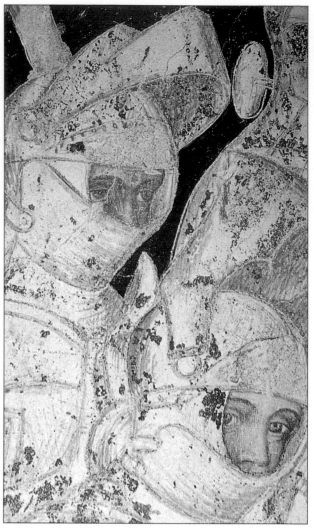

*Details of the
jousting scenes
of the* Tournament of
Louverzep, *by
Pisanello.*

as to the date. We know that Pisanello was in Mantua frequently in the years between 1422 and 1442 (although some authors maintain that it was 1442 and 1447), also creating medals for the Gonzaga; his work in Mantua as a painter was soon forgotten, except for a document which mentions that the ceiling of the "Sala di Pisanello" collapsed in 1480, but it was not certain which room was referred to. This cycle does not simply repeat the Breton stories, but has been adapted by Pisanello to include various motifs that allude to the Gonzaga court, such as the dog looking backwards, the small deer, and above all the collars with the swan pendant in honor of the emblem bestowed on the Duke in 1436 by King Henry IV of England or by the Hohenzollern later (the family of Barbara of Brandenburg, in which case the cycle would have to date to after 1444). Subsequent decoration had hidden Pisanello's work in this room, and for all we know even today there may be other fine cycles under the ornamentation of the tens of kilometers of walls in the palace.

Details of the sinopias, by Pisanello.

In the past years restoration of the Arthurian frescoes has furnished new and important information. Pisanello's technique was mainly fresco and the cycle was never finished in the layout of the stories. The painter actually interrupted his work, leaving the red sinopia preparatory sketches fully visible. The main surviving fresco fragment shows knights with their horses at rest (although some detached pieces have not yet been interpreted). A figure with a gilded arabesqued turban stands out at the center of a group of gentlemen. The horses are carefully executed, particularly the hoofs and nostrils.

Appartamento Verde (Green Apartment)

The Salette dell'Alcova lead to the so-called Galleria Nuova, which was originally built overlook-

Apartment of Tapestries (School of Raphael, 16th cent.).

ing the *Cortile d'Onore* or courtyard as an open loggia at the beginning of the seventeenth century by Viani, and later transformed into an exhibition space at the end of the eighteenth century by Paolo Pozzo. To be noted here in particular are a canvas with *Scenes from the Life of St. John the Evangelist*, by Girolamo Mazzola Bedoli (1500-1569), a *Flagellation and Deposition* by Lorenzo Costa the Younger (1537-1583) and finally a *Presentation of Mary in the Temple* by Domenico Fetti (1589-1623), one of the principal figures in painting in Mantua in the sixteenth century.

Next comes the *Appartamento degli Arazzi* (Apartment of Tapestries), which also overlooks the courtyard, completely furnished in 1779-80 on a project by Paolo Pozzo and with rich pictorial and plastic decoration by Stanislao Somazzi and Giovanni Battista Marconi, reflecting the Neoclassic taste of the Austrian rulers in Mantua, who chose this wing of the palace as their headquarters (many stuccoes were modelled directly on Roman sarcophagi, to make them seem more authentic). Nine tapestries of the Flemish school woven in Brussels around 1530 on cartoons by Raphael, and which arrived in Mantua shortly after the middle of the century, hang on the walls. These are early copies of the famous series in

the Vatican Library, the cartoons for which are now in the Victoria and Albert Museum in London. The subjects are taken from the lives of Saint Peter and Saint Paul as narrated in the New Testament: the first room contains the *Healing of the Lame Man* (note the two large twisted columns which frame the main scene in the foreground: these are the so-called "Solomonic" columns, which echo in shape the architectural orders in the Cortile della Rustica), the *Sacrifice of Lystri* (which took place in Lystri, a town in Asia Minor), and the *Death of Ananias*; the second room contains the *Conversion of Saint Paul*, the *Saint Preaching in Athens*, and then the *Primacy of Peter*, one of the finest.

Next comes the Passetto, which originally served as the Chapel, with the barrel vault frescoed by Lorenzo Costa the Younger; the next room contains other Raphael tapestries such as the *Miraculous Draught of Fishes* (the finest of them), the *Blinding of the Magician Elymas*, who opposed St. Paul's preaching, and finally the *Martyrdom of Saint Stephen* who had defended Jesus.

In the Sala dello Zodiaco, the walls, redone in Neoclassic style by dal Pozzo, are in sharp contrast to the *Signs of the Zodiac*, and in particular *Night*, painted on the ceiling in 1579 by Lorenzo Costa the Younger.

Left:
Apartment of Tapestries, Miraculous Draught of Fishes *(detail).*

Below:
ceiling of the Sala dello Zodiaco (on the vault, Night*).*

Above:
*view of the
Salone dei
Fiumi.*

Right:
*detail of the
central doorway
in the hall.*

Next comes the scenic Salone dei Fiumi (Hall of Rivers), built as a loggia in 1575 for Guglielmo Gonzaga and, richly decorated around 1780 in a style that was still basically late-Baroque: the two grottoes with marble vases, set at either end, date to the late seventeenth century.

The left wall of the room is articulated in trompe l'oeil panels, with painted pergola openings which echo the large symmetrical windows overlooking the Hanging Garden. The allegorical personifications of the *Rivers* which run through the territory of the old Gonzaga dukedom were painted by Giorgio Anselmi (1723-1797), assisted by Gaetano Crevola (known between 1758 and 1794). Anselmi also painted the decoration of the vault with *Phaeton Asking for the Chariot of the Sun.*

Views of the Hanging Garden.

Giardino Pensile (Hanging Garden)

Between 1579 and 1580 Guglielmo Gonzaga had the architect Pompeo Pedemonte (1515-1592) systematize the approximately square space for the Hanging Garden (the old Giardino in Aria), with a portico on three sides and closed by a wing, where the Sala dei Fiumi is located, on the fourth. The left side looks down on Piazza Sordello, a good twelve meters below, and is set on powerful supporting structures (an aerial passageway that led directly to the Cathedral, right opposite, began here). The formal qualities, with coupled Tuscan columns supporting the arcading, and the underlying concept of a secret Italian-style garden, would seem to indicate that it was designed by Giovan Battista Bertani, who was the architect of the ducal construction yards for years, prior to Pedemonte. To the right of the Garden is the so-called Cortile delle Otto Facce, with a singular layout dating to 1582 This would seem to indicate that the last enlargement of the Ducal Palace on Piazza Sordello was a single complex, composed of the Garden and the Court, closing the Corte Vecchia on the north. It was built by Bernardino Faciotto who used arcading with smooth-faced rustication at the bottom while the walls above must have been frescoed or at least decorated with a facing that was never carried out. In 1773, a "Kaffeehaus" was built in the Garden on the site of the sixteenth-century ice house on the side across from the present Galleria dei Fiumi. This kiosk with a pierced vault was highly scenographic and therefore probably designed by Antonio Galli Bibiena, at work on other prestigious buildings in the city. The architect used the same type of theatrical approach in the Church of Santa Maria Assunta in Sabbioneta, also previously employed by Gaetano Ghidetti (presumably however at the suggestion of Antonio) in the vault of the church of Sant'Antonio Abate in Parma, built on a project by Ferdinando Galli Bibiena. Inside, the lower part of the Kaffeehaus is decorated with fine polychrome marbles from the Palazzo del Giardino in Sabbioneta.

smooth-faced rustication initially supported an open gallery (later closed on all four sides and replaced, on the south side, by the Loggia Nuova).

Appartamento dell'Imperatrice
(Apartment of the Empress)

This three-room apartment was built to a design by Paolo Pozzo in 1778 for sovereigns and princesses who were passing through. It was subsequently taken over by the archduchess Beatrice d'Este, consort of the Governor of Lombardy, Ferdinand of Hapsburg-Lorraine. In 1811 Eugène de Beauharnais lived there, and refurbished it (the furniture there now dates to that time).

Appartamento dei duchi Guglielmo e Vincenzo
Cortile d'Onore (Courtyard)

The large space known as the *Cortile d'Onore* (or Giardino Ducale) is the result of various renovations dating primarily to between the sixteenth and the seventeenth centuries: the west wing (that is parallel to Piazza Sordello) probably dates to around 1520, when Isabella d'Este had her new apartments (known as del Giardino) installed in two fifteenth-century wings of the Corte Vecchia. The courtyard was reorganized and the facades were unified at the beginning of the seventeenth century. The portico below in

Sala dei Falconi (Room of the Falcons)

The Sala dei Falconi or Room of the Falcons, commissioned by Guglielmo around 1580, is located between the Cortile delle Otto Facce and the Cortile d'Onore. It was remodelled by Vincenzo in the early seventeenth century and once more redesigned in the Neoclassic period, as were most of the rooms in this apartment.

The decoration on the vault, with *Putti and falcons playing*, is by Ippolito Andreasi (1548-1608), while on the walls are paintings of the *Notables* of the Gonzaga court in the sixteenth and seventeenth centuries.

Saletta dei Mori (Room of the Moors)

The room is characterized by the ceiling and frieze below with Moors and caryatids (female figures serving as supports for the horizontals above), in carved and gilded walnut in Venetian style. On the walls are sixteenth- and seventeenth-century paintings, including a sixteenth-century copy, with variations, of the *Madonna with the Pearl* now in Madrid, attributed to Giulio Romano.

Galleria degli Specchi (Hall of Mirrors)

The six oil paintings of *Martyr Saints* hung in the Loggetta dei Mori are by Domenico Fetti and date to the early seventeenth century. The Corridoio dei Mori, also seventeenth century, was decorated for Ferdinando (1613-1626) with stuccowork, medallions and grotesques. The corridor leads to the Galleria degli Specchi or Hall of Mirrors, originally an open gallery overlooking the courtyard, designed by Antonio Maria Viani for Vincenzo I in the early seventeenth century and used as a space for receptions and musical gatherings (at right angles is the Galleria Nuova, also designed by Viani but finished inside in the eighteenth century). The frescoes in the vaulted ceiling and lunettes are by artists active at the court of

Preceding page, above: *Cortile d'Onore (Courtyard)*; below: *decorated ceiling in the* *Room of the Falcons.*

Above: *Hall of Mirrors.*

Mantua when Ferdinando was duke, such as Francesco Borgani (1557-1624), while the walls were redone in Neoclassic style, and the mirrors were added after 1779, by Giocondo Albertolli. The various mythological and allegorical scenes and calculated optical effects make this amazing and magnificent hall, repainted in the eighteenth century by Felice Campi (1746-1817), one of the most fascinating in the entire Palace, a sort of perfect fusion between the artistic demands of the sixteenth and eighteenth centuries, mediated by the seventeenth-century marble busts of *Princesses*. To be noted in particular in the vaulting are the scene of *Olympus* and the *Chariots of Day and Night* which sources attribute to pupils of Guido Reni (in line, therefore, with the penetrating perspective studies of Bolognese "*quadraturismo*") as well as artists of the grand coloristic late Mannerist style of Bavaria.

Right:
Hall of Mirrors, vault fresco with the Chariots of Day and Night *(17th cent.) by F. Gessi and G. Sementi (detail).*

Below, left to right:
Corbels in the Room of the Bowmen (detail); Martyrdom of Saint'Ursula, *(attributed to P. P. Rubens), (16th cent.).*

To be noted in particular is the perspective illusion which makes the horses of the chariots at the sides, seem to have "turned" when one has reached the other end of the Gallery, or the index finger of the woman at the center of the wall which seems to be pointed at the visitor from beginning to end.

Salone degli Arcieri *(Room of the Bowmen)*

This was originally a large antechamber, named after the duke's personal bodyguards, where the visitors waited to be admitted to the presence of Vincenzo Gonzaga. Finished around 1620 on a design by Viani who unified two floors of the old building, the hall has an interesting ceiling supported by large corbels with female figures of the caryatid type. The panels painted with horses behind curtains are attributed to Viani, while a large painting was to decorate the center of the ceiling (which comes from the palazzo of San Sebastiano). The room contains the painting of the *Gonzaga Family in Adoration of the Trinity*, by Peter Paul Rubens (1577-1640), dating to 1605 and originally in the church of the SS. Trinità in

Mantua, from which it was taken and cut into pieces in Napoleonic times.

Other interesting works include a bozzetto by Rubens of the *Martyrdom of Sant'Ursula*, while the *Nativity of the Virgin* is by the school of Tintoretto (1518-1594) (at present in restoration), and the *Multiplication of Loaves and Fish* by Domenico Fetti (1589-1623).

Above:
The Gonzaga
Family in
Adoration,
*by P.P. Rubens,
(1605).*

Left:
*Sala di
Giuditta, fresco
showing* Judith
at the Camp of
Holofernes
*by P. Menghi
(17th cent.).*

Sala di Giuditta *(Room of Judith)*

This room was part of the private apartments of Vincenzo I, reorganized by Viani. The eighteenth-century canvases of the *Life of Judith*, by Pietro Menghi are rather interesting, while most of the other works by various artists on the walls date to Vincenzo's time, as does the ceiling decorated with the duke's heraldic emblem (a crucible in which golden rods are being tested by fire). This ceiling, too, comes from the palace of San Sebastiano, near Palazzo Te, and was installed here by Viani.

Room of the Labyrinth, wooden ceiling in a labyrinth pattern, from the Palazzo di S. Sebastiano. On the walls, The Age of Gold, *by Sante Peranda, (16th cent.).*

Sala del Labirinto *(Room of the Labyrinth)*

The Sala del Labirinto takes its name from the fact that the ceiling (which also comes from the palazzo of San Sebastiano) is decorated with a fine labyrinth, a golden path between walls of green shrubbery, like the labyrinths to be found in Renaissance gardens. Each green stretch bears the words *"forse che sì, forse che no"* (maybe yes, maybe no), later used by Gabriele D'Annunzio, the famous Italian poet and novelist, as the title of a novel published in 1910, some of which was set in Mantua. All around is a band, added when the panels were reassembled, with an inscription which recalls the struggle of Vincenzo against the Turks at Canizza in Voivodina (1601), while the motto would refer to the duke's indecision as to whether to participate in this battle or not. The canvases on the walls and the frieze, with depictions of the *Ages of the World*, are by Palma the Younger (1544-1628) and Sante Peranda (1566-1638), who also painted the portraits below (all of Peranda's works come from the Castle of the Pico Dukes in Mirandola).

Sala del Crogiuolo *(Room of the Crucible)*

This room is characterized by its rich ceiling and a frieze (once more from the palazzo of San Sebastiano, as were the ceilings of the neighboring rooms).

The name of course refers to the crucibles shown here. The frieze panels with *Putti and Dogs* were painted by Lorenzo Costa the Younger in the time of Guglielmo for the Stanza dello Zodiaco and were reassembled here in 1922. On the walls are portraits of the Pico di Mirandola family, also by Sante Peranda.

Sala di Amore e Psiche *(Room of Cupid and Psyche)*

The Sala di Amore e Psiche, originally seventeenth century, was completely renovated in the Neoclassic period, when the tondo with *Cupid and Psyche* was set into the center of the ceiling (covering a papal coat of arms beneath).

On the walls are paintings by Giuseppe Bazzani, a leading figure of Mantuan painting in the first half of the eighteenth century, and by Lucrina Fetti, Domenico's sister.

Next come the *Saletta dei Quattro Elementi* with four paintings by Giorgio Anselmi (1723-1797), the most important painter in Mantua in the second half of the eighteenth century. The oval portrait of *Maria Theresa of Austria*, also by Anselmi, was one of the paintings hung in the principal rooms of the Palace

under the Hapsburgs. The *Sala di Giove e Giunone*, originally Guglielmo's private chapel in the sixteenth century, has canvases by Giuseppe Maria Crespi (1665-1747) and Carlo Bononi (1569-1632). The room is named after the painting on the ceiling of *Jupiter and Juno*. Next comes the *Sala di Leda*, named after the goddess shown on the ceiling, after which comes the Stufetta, a tiny room, a sort of heated study, with a fine coffered ceiling with gilding on a blue ground and rich inlays.

Room of Cupid and Psyche, paintings of the 18th cent.

Above:
*Saletta dei
Quattro
Elementi.*

Below: *facade
of Fancelli's
Domus
(15th cent.)*

*and the
Botanical
Garden.*

Domus Nova (or Appartamento di Eleonora dei Medici) and the Giardino del Padiglione
(Domus Nova and Pavilion Garden)

The complex of the *Domus Nova* was in a sense created by gemmation of the medieval nucleus of the original Gonzaga palace which faced on Piazza Sordello, towards the east and the Lago Inferiore. The project drawn up by Luca Fancelli and begun in 1480 was for a rectangular court closed by four wings, of which the fourth side on Piazzale della Palace (now Piazza Lega Lombarda) was never completed, forming a U-shaped space.

The east wing, at present housing the offices of the *Soprintendenza ai Beni Artistici e Storici di Mantova, Brescia e Cremona*, known as *Ala del Paradiso*, was designed as the *Apartment of Eleonora dei Medici*, on the occasion of her marriage to the duke Vincenzo in 1584. To be noted in the apartment are the two *Salette delle Città* with plans of Italian cities and a series of interesting stucco ornaments; and the *Stanza dei Quattro Elementi* based on prints published by Antonio Tempesta at the beginning of the seventeenth century.

Towards the Lago Inferiore, and therefore across from the *Cortile del Padiglione*, in which a Botanical Garden was installed at the beginning of the seventeenth century, is the original facade of the complex, designed by Luca Fancelli after 1480 as the principal facade of the Palace on the east, on the lake (it was completed during the 1942 restoration of the Palace). This is the only example in Mantua of the canonic superimposition of the architectural orders, in this case of pilasters subdivided in two tiers, in line with the dictates of Leon Battista Alberti.

It is moreover also an interesting case of the adoption of pilasters of the giant order on the facade of a private building, embracing two levels in height, once more reflecting Alberti's ideas, since Fancelli was his pupil and head of Alberti's construction yards in the city.

Originally there was a nymphaeum covered by a pavilion (or Padiglione) in the court (from which it gets its name), built in 1581 by Bernardino Facciotto, and then replaced in 1680 by a *scena pubblica* for the theater (the Corridor which led to the Teatro Vecchio, which has been demolished, is still there).

Corridoio del Bertani or of Santa Barbara (Bertani's Corridor)

The corridor may have been designed by Bertani, although construction was not begun until 1581, after his death. Something was needed to provide a direct route between the "Fancelliani" rooms of the Corte Vecchia and the Castle of San Giorgio, without having to pass through all the apartments of the "Corte Nuova".

The sixteenth-century additions to the Ducal Palace made it absolutely necessary to redesign the various routes and make them more functional.

This complex is of particular interest for it was more than a simple aerial passageway, and contained collections of paintings. In 1627 it was known as the "Corridore dei Quadri" ("Picture Corridor"). Originally it was closed above by a continuous terrace with a balustrade, known as the "Terrazza delle Dame" (now replaced by a roof) from which the notables of the court watched the events that took place in the Castle Courtyard.

After descending the ramp leading to the Corridor one turns right.

Appartamento dei Nani or the Scala Santa (Apartment of the Dwarfs)

A wing to the right of the Corridoio del Bertani leads to the Appartamento dei Nani or Scala Santa, below the Appartamento Ducale of Fancelli's Domus Nova, and which has traditionally been considered, because it is so small, as an Apartment for Dwarfs, also called of Paradise since it is in the wing of that name. Recently the devotional nature of this series of rooms has come to the fore, as a miniaturized version of the complex of the Scala Santa in Rome. This was built for the duke, Ferdinando Gonzaga, formerly a cardinal, as a large reliquary and was inaugurated in 1615: the nucleus consists of an octagonal room (the Reliquary), the point of arrival after having passed through the other rooms on one's knees.

Corte Nuova (New Court)

In the course of the sixteenth century the Palace was considerably enlarged on the side overlooking the Lago Inferiore and in the areas that were still free between the nucleus of the Corte Vecchia and the Castle of San Giorgio. Important wings were added to the Gonzaga residence, beginning with the commissions entrusted by the Marchesi to Giulio Romano, who arrived in the city in 1524.

Many of these were probably only designed by the architect and then built by the man who succeeded him in his post, Giovan Battista Bertani, who was the man responsible for the general aspect of the Corte Nuova today. Giulio Romano was in charge of the building of the so-called *Rustica* (overlooking the Lago Inferiore), the renovations in the apartments around the *Cortile dei Cani*, as well as the *Palazzina della Paleologa* (adjoining the Castle, but then destroyed in the nineteenth century).

Work was still in progress when he died in 1546 and continuation of the projects was turned over to his pupil Giovan Battista Bertani, who had been collaborating with the Master at least as early as 1531.

Bertani may have been entrusted with the completion of the *Cortile della Mostra* (called of the *Cavallerizza* ever since the eighteenth century, and designed by Giulio Romano) in 1549.

The Courtyard joined the apartments known respectively as "Estivale" (or Rustica) and "di Troia". He also created a series of further important structures behind Giulio Romano's buildings, such as the palatine church of Santa Barbara, the Corridor which directly connected the castle of San Giorgio to the Corte Vecchia, the large courtyard known as Prato di Castello, as well as a new entrance to the complex by transforming a precedent ephemeral apparatus of his own design.

His work was completed by Antonio Maria Viani who turned his hand to making many of the rooms more functional, built passages that joined them, refurnished the apartments in seventeenth-century taste, when it was decided to make the palace more magnificent.

In the eighteenth century Paolo Pozzo and a series of artists in the circle of the civic Academy of Fine Arts once more refurbished the rooms, concentrating on the sculptural and pictorial decoration in line with the new tastes in art.

Appartamento della Metamorfosi or Galleria del Passerino
(Apartment of the Metamorphosis)

The Appartamento della Metamorfosi is comprised of a series of four rooms, three of which are decorated on the ceiling with representations in the frieze and ceilings, framed by stuccoes, from the stories of the *Metamorphoses* by the Latin author Ovid, as illustrated by Antonio Tempesta in the edition published in Antwerp in 1606 (just as the images of the *Four Elements* in the Stanza dei Quattro Elementi in the neighboring *Appartamento di Eleonora dei Medici* were also taken from prints by Tempesta).

Although Vincenzo had commissioned this apartment from Viani in 1594-95, it was not realized until the second decade of the seventeenth century. These rooms were designed to hold the duke's naturalistic collections (also called "*Stanze dei Quattro Elementi*": earth, water, air and fire), in other words a sort of *Wunderkammer* or room of marvels where the duke kept his collection of strange, petrified, rare, monstrous objects and even the embalmed body of Passerino Bonacolsi (fundamental for the survival of the Gonzaga dynasty for it was believed that their rule over Mantua would last as long as they had the body of Passerino. In the eighteenth century the body was lost in the course of moving and this is supposedly why the Gonzaga were expelled from the city). The Gallery contains antique marbles including a first century B.C. relief with a *Battle between Gauls and Romans*. This piece is particularly important for it was one of the things Giulio Romano brought to Mantua along with his "bric-a-brac". The artist had already used the figure composition as inspiration for the Battle to be found in the Hall of Constantine in the Vatican, while the same model was later reproposed, freely, here in the Ducal Palace by Romano in the scene of the *Battle for the Body of Patrocles* in the *Sala di Troia*.

La Rustica or Appartamento Estivale
(Summer Apartment)

Designed by Giulio Romano and completed by Bertani, this apartment was subjected to changes in later centuries and it is hard to say just what it looked like when Giulio Romano and Bertani had finished with it. The complex consists of three distinct parts, with the one overlooking the Pavilion courtyard undoubtedly later, and to be tied in with the work of Antonio Maria Viani.

The first room, with rich stucco decorations, is known as *Camera degli Amori di Giove (Room of*

Jupiter's Loves), from the themes in the lunettes. Then comes the *Camerino di Orfeo* with four stucco panels, treated like cameos in their light coloring on a dark background, and above all with a fresco relating to the *Story of Orpheus*. Then comes the *Stanza dei Pesci* or di *Nettuno* with paintings attributed to Lorenzo Costa the Younger, with shells and aquatic groups. The next room, the *Sala dei Frutti*, is the main room in the apartment, perhaps originally a loggia and then decorated by Lorenzo Costa with episodes and personages of the *Story of Mantua*, framed in the smaller panels by garlands of fruit. Virgil's *History of Mantua* has been interpreted from a sixteenth-century point of view. An example is the *Legend of Manto*, here considered the heroine of that name, that is the founder of the city. To be noted are the episodes of the *Founding of Mantua* and the *Construction of the City Gates*.

The apartment also has other rooms including the *Salone delle Quattro Colonne* and that of the *Due Colonne*, which must once have had particularly interesting painted architectural elements of which very little remains.

On the ground floor there is a room in which *Putti playing under a pergola supported by twisted columns* are painted. The subject is of note as an example of the frequent use by Giulio Romano and his school (as well as his followers) of this specific architectural motif of the twisted column which lent itself to two different interpretations. As a religious motif, it was the "Solomonic" column, of Biblical origin. As such it appears, for example, in Raphael's tapestry of the *Healing of the Lame Man* on the walls of the Appartamento Verde here in the Ducal Palace (which, incidentally, the Gonzaga bought in 1559) or Giulio Romano's *Circumcision* now in the Louvre. As a rustic element, its curious shape made it suitable for garden pavilions and grottoes, such as here and in the adjoining Cortile della Cavallerizza (on the other hand, this preference of Raphael and Giulio for the twisted column also conditioned, aside from Bertani, the text by Cristoforo Sorte, *Sulla Pittura*, published in 1584).

Il Cortile della Cavallerizza (Cavalry Courtyard)

The Cortile della Cavallerizza, called "Cortile della Mostra" ("Exhibition Courtyard") in the sixteenth century, has long been entirely attributed in concept to Giulio Romano, while today, on the basis of various documents, only the facade of the complex known as "la Rustica", on the south side, is considered to be by Romano. The "Corritore discoperto" overlooking the lake which joins la Rustica with the building on the other side of the court, also designed by Giulio, is now attributed to Giovan Battista Bertani. In the fifteenth century, various buildings stood on the fourth side, where the Galleria della Mostra now is. These were then unified by Viani. Bertani however may already have considered creating a general conformity by adding a facade that resembled the others, like the one there today.

As far as la Rustica is concerned we know that work for this side of the Court was begun in 1538-39, while the *Appartamento di Troia* across from it was being finished. The complex, facing east towards the lake so it would be particularly comfortable during the hot summer months (hence the name of "Appartamento Estivale" or Summer Apartment), overlooks a courtyard. The facade has an open porti-

co below with piers of rusticated ashlars, which must originally have also framed the garden furnishings, "brooks and fountains" (Giulio Romano had designed this portico with wide bays so it could withstand the flooding of the lake). The floors above have an unusual order of half columns with twisted grooved shaft, suited for gardens, while the capitals of these engaged columns and the entablature are of the

Cortile della Cavallerizza (Courtyard of the Cavalry Apartment), with the bell-tower of the Palatine Basilica of S. Barbara in the background, (16th cent.).

Doric order, used by Romano in the Courtyard of the Palazzo Te. It had been thought that Giulio's design initially consisted of only three bays, but the fact that the ashlars are homogeneous and their arrangement perfectly symmetrical to the central axis, means that the present complete facade follows Giulio Romano's design, to which many structural and formal details bear witness. The window jambs on the other hand are possibly by Bertani and are therefore later.

Bertani's intervention would date to between 1549 and 1556, the year in which the curtain wall of the "*Corritore*" overlooking the lake was finished after an old fortification wall had been torn down. The curtain wall was particularly scenographic with a double alternation of arches and windows (an articulation of openings that may be related to that of an ancient Roman aqueduct), but which was completely lacking in decorative details on the outer side, stressing the fact that this was by no means to be thought of as a new facade for the palace, and that the elegance of the architecture was so to say introvert. Bertani thus apparently simply repeated the articulation of Giulio Romano's facade for la Rustica in the other facades of the Court, transforming and enlarging the Loggia which originally faced out on the Castle side in correspondence to the *Appartamento di Troia*, to form a Gallery (the present Galleria dei Mesi).

The Court, which could be covered, if necessary, by a large protective canopy, as in the Roman amphitheaters, was used for parades, tournaments, while the surrounding lake was used for court ephemera such as naval battles, (*naumachie*), fireworks which were watched from the open "*Corritore*". It was not until the eighteenth century that the Mostra was used as a manège, hence the name Cortile della Cavallerizza or Cavalry Courtyard, and at this time the wooden roof designed by Francesco Galli Bibiena was built.

La Galleria della Mostra (Exhibition Gallery)

Between 1592 and 1612, Vincenzo had his architect, Giovan Antonio Viani, complete the long Galleria della Mostra (about seventy-seven meters long by seven wide) to close the fourth side of the Cortile della Mostra, begun in 1590 by the architect Dattari. It is of course possible that Giulio Romano or Bertani had already planned for the construction of this courtyard which was also closed in on the west, that is towards the interior of the Palazzo. The gallery was to house part of the duke's collections of art and archaeology. Viani unified a series of buildings and rooms that were already extant, basing himself for the

Right:
Galleria della Mostra (Exhibition Gallery).

Facing page:
Galleria dei Mesi or dei Marmi (Gallery of the Months or of Marble Sculpture).

facade on the architectural idiom used previously by Giulio Romano, and then Bertani, for the other three sides. Inside he created a two-story space, which was also lit by the windows of the attic above (closed however on the other sides of the Cortile). A series of exceptional Roman portraits are still to be seen in the large niches in the Gallery, once closed by doors (while much of the ceiling is the result of the 1934 restoration and many busts are copies).

Appartamento di Troia or of Duke Federico II
(Apartment of Troy or of Duke Federico II)

From 1536 to 1539, Giulio Romano was engaged in overseeing the building of this new Apartment known originally as "di Castello", because it was adjacent to the Castle of San Giorgio, and later "di Troia", after the scenes of the Trojan war in the main hall. Of particular interest in their pertinent reference to the antique, are the barrel vaults in all these rooms (with the exception of the Camera dei Cavalli) which were meant to house the duke's collections of antiquities: a sort of direct correspondence between the objects and their architectural container. Installation was still in progress in 1574 when a a visit by King Henry II of France forced Guglielmo, who lived in these wings, to move to the Corte Vecchia. Previously Bertani had already modified Giulio Romano's original idea of a loggia overlooking the Cortile della Mostra. Bertani closed in the loggia and transformed it into a Gallery, now known as the Galleria dei Marmi or dei Mesi (to be noted that at present not a single piece of the antique sculpture originally there is left). The entrance to the entire apartment was shifted to the *Sala di Manto*, while other rooms, not in Giulio's original plans, were added to the complex, modifying the original feeling for space and light.

Galleria dei Mesi or dei Marmi
(Gallery of the Months or of Marble Sculpture)

The Loggia dei Mesi, initially with three bays, was built to designs by Giulio Romano, as an open loggia with an apse at either end (1538-39). The name derives from the stucco and fresco decorations on the walls. The stucco putti in the arches of the first bays hold the *Signs of the Zodiac* (therefore the months). In 1573, Guglielmo had this loggia doubled in length and closed by Bertani, who used Giulio's facade for la Rustica, opposite, as his model for the new outer facade overlooking the Cortile della Cavallerizza. The result was a real gallery for the duke's collection of classic marble sculpture: the first gallery in the palace,

called "dei Marmi", in accordance with the latest French fashion of galleries, but set up as a real museum - one of the first of its kind - with niches for antiquities and with reliefs in the various panels. The interior of this vast room is characterized by its sumptuous decoration: the architectural order of pilasters on pedestals frames, on the right wall, windows (which replaced the original open arches) and on the left, the niches which contained marble busts.

The end walls, only one of which is derived from Giulio's design, are hollowed out in large niches set under half domes. The gallery has an antique style barrel vault, while the decorations are all derived from classical sources with putti, victory figures, vine scrolls and grotesques, motifs already adopted in Rome in the circle of Raphael, Giulio Romano's master, and then taken up again by the artists working with Bertani.

To be noted in the gallery, at the east end in the panels over the doors, marble bas-reliefs of Augustan period, in particular, the *Throne of Jupiter*, which Giulio Romano completed by inserting a stucco figure of the cup-bearer of the Gods, *Ganymede*. The finest piece of the present collection is however an antique marble of Hadrianic period depicting an

Amazonomachy (with a few additions probably by Giulio), where in three large groups of five figures each, the Amazons are shown battling the Greeks, with the dead and restive horses all around. Originally Giulio Romano had set this relief over one of the two entrances to the *Appartamento di Troia* (a relief of Antonine date was over the other). Antique pieces were in fact to be found throughout the Palazzo, an indication of the richness of the Gonzaga collection which included many pieces that had belonged to the Marchesa Isabella, to Andrea Mantegna and to Giulio Romano himself. Most of this marvelous collection was taken as loot or sold between 1626 and 1711. Today the pieces on exhibit come mostly from the Antiquarium of Sabbioneta which belonged to Vespasiano Gonzaga.

After the Galleria dei Mesi comes the *Loggia di Eleonora*, from which an enchanting view of the Lago Inferiore can be had: to be noted the Medici coats of arms of the duchess and the Gonzaga devices of the duke, Vincenzo.

Sala di Troia *(Room of Troy)*

While the less important rooms of the Appartamento are decorated with figures taken from a naturalistic repertory (birds, horses, etc.), the Sala di Troia, originally used as the Audience Hall, was sumptuously decorated by Giulio Romano and his workshop between 1536 and 1539 with scenes of the Trojan war inspired by Homer's epic. Archaeological details and antique motifs abound. The figures of gods stand out on the ceiling and on the walls, rather aloof, while it is the Greek heroes such as *Achilles and Diomedes*, rather than the Trojan heroes, who are exalted, in line with the philo-Hellenic program worked out by Benedetto Lampridio as an allegorical celebration of the political role of Federico Gonzaga and of Mantua as a new Olympus. The glorification of the Gonzaga family was in fact closely connected to that of the Greeks after Margherita Paleologo, from an eminent Byzantine family, married the duke in 1531. To be noted on the walls are, from left to right, the *Rape of Helen*, the *Dream of Hecuba*, the *Judgement of Paris*. At the back are the *Construction of the Trojan Horse, Vulcan making Weapons for Achilles, Laocoon and his Sons Attacked by Marine Serpents* and *Aias Oileus Struck Down on the Reef*. On the ceiling is the representation of Olympus, with the Gods divided in support of the Greeks or the Trojans, whom they surround in the battle scenes taken from the story of the *Iliad*. The *Battle over the Body of Patrocles* was modelled on an antique piece of sculpture brought to Mantua by Giulio Romano, now on exhibit in the *Appartamento delle Metamorfosi* (or

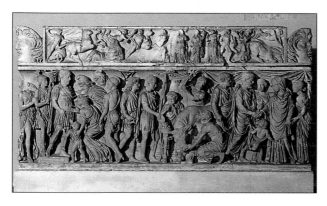

Preceding page: *Room of Troy.*

Above: *Room of Troy,* Sacrifice of the Bull, *Roman*

sarcophagus (2nd cent. A.D.).

Galleria del Passerino). There were once cupboards below which contained objects of exceptional artistic value that belonged to the Gonzaga collection, unfortunately also now dispersed.

Camera delle Teste and Gabinetto dei Cesari (Room of the Heads and Cabinet of the Emperors)

The Camera delle Teste and the Gabinetto dei Cesari (of the Caesars or Emperors) are two rooms with closely related iconographic programs. In the first, a series of busts "in antique style" celebrated Gonzaga ancestors, allies and military captains (the names are still visible on the surviving bases) in the form of a classic repertory of figures. At the center of the ceiling is the image of *Jupiter,* with whom Federico identified, drawing a parallel between his lofty role and that of the Father of the Gods who overshadows even the greatest *condottieri* (the inscription is the same as that on a medal of one of the duke's ancestors). The two fragments of mural oil paintings with *Victories Writing* are attributed to Giulio Romano.

At the side, in the Gabinetto dei Cesari (cited also by Vasari), the glorification of the Gonzaga line achieved one of its climaxes with the eleven Roman emperors (now in late sixteenth or early seventeenth-century copies) painted by Titian in 1537. The cycle was originally designed for the Loggia of David in the Palazzo Te. In 1531, Federico had asked Paolo Giovio to provide him with descriptions for the portraits of the emperors, on the basis of an archaeological taste which derived the aspect and features "in part from medals, in part from antique marbles". Paintings by Giulio Romano completed the Sala, in which decoration and painting combined to create a room of great formal quality, together with the bronze and marble sculpture set in niches with grotesques (in keeping with the Renaissance concept of the Antiquarium-Museum).

Camerino dei Falconi (Small Falcon Room)

In the ceiling, from which unfortunately the falcons have disappeared, the Camerino dei Falconi still has a fine stucco tondo at the center with the *Rape of Ganymede* (the cartoon of this scene by Giulio Romano is now in New York) and two scenes depicting respectively *Tarquinius and Lucretia* and the *Myth of Ippo,* who committed suicide rather than being raped by pirates. There used to be pilaster strips on the wall framing areas which contained pictures of mythological subjects (now scattered in various collections and museums).

Camera dei Cavalli (Room of the Horses)

In the Camera dei Cavalli, rebuilt in 1536 on pre-existent structures, Giulio Romano adopted various devices in his ornamental plan aimed at eliminating the irregularity of the walls so that the trapezoidal plan of the room would appear to be more symmetrical. He therefore used cornices that varied in width and decoration, employing the laws of perspective to make things look regular; these expedients were also used in the ceiling with coffers of different shapes and size. In 1536, Isabella d'Este, who had commissioned the work, "entrò in la Camera di Cavalli ch'è finita, li paresse cossa tanto bella, che non si potrà satiare laudare-ella". ("entered the Camera dei Cavalli which is finished, it seemed so beautiful to her, that she could not praise it enough") Giulio's paintings of *Horses* which decorated the room are no longer there, while the canvas at the center of the ceiling, unquestionably designed by Giulio for the entrance to the *Appartamento di Troia,* was installed in 1928. The *Fall of Icarus* by Giulio Romano is at the center of the ceiling, while interesting still lifes, with fruit and vegetables, some of the first of the kind, are in the corner ceiling coffers.

Appartamento Grande or of Duke Guglielmo
(Large Apartment or of Duke Guglielmo)

The apartment of Guglielmo adjoins the Appartamento di Troia and looks out on the *Cortile detto dei Cani* (*Courtyard of the Dogs*), designed as a hanging garden (the name comes from a plaque honoring "Oriana, cagnolina celeste" or "Oriana, heavenly little dog") with outer walls which, like those of the Loggetta degli Grotteschi, were originally painted. Work was begun in 1572 by Giovan Battista Bertani who remodeled some of Giulio's rooms. Completed by 1580, this became one of the most sumptuous apartments in the palace, further enriched by Vincenzo who used it for the most elaborate court fêtes (like the one in 1584 on the occasion of his wedding). Even during the subsequent Austrian rule this apartment remained one of the most important in the entire complex.

Sala di Manto (Room of Manto)

In 1527 Bertani transformed a series of late fifteenth-century rooms into an entrance to the new ducal Apartment through the Scalone di Enea nearby. The Hall, used for receptions and fêtes, takes its name from the eight figural panels, separated by pilaster strips, done in oil by Lorenzo Costa the Younger, an unusual technique for murals. The scenes refer to the legendary founding of Mantua by Manto, daughter of the seer Teiresias, as told by the classic authors and elaborated by the men of learning at the Gonzaga court in the second half of the sixteenth century. Guglielmo had *Manto's Landing* and *Manto's Banquet* shown, while other scenes are in poor condition and hard to interpret.

The wooden ceiling, which unified the space, is also of note as are the antique statues now here, including the *Apollo of Mantua*, Roman copy of a fifth-century B.C. Greek original.

Preceding page: *Room of Manto.*

Left: Federigo II Encloses the City in Walls *(detail).*

Below, left: Apollo of Mantua; right: *Sala dei Marchesi (detail).*

The apartment continues with a series of rooms with iconography celebrating the Gonzaga dynasty, such as the Sala dei Capitani (the ceiling is attributed to Bertani), while among the allegorical stucco figures in the Camera dei Marchesi (built from scratch by 1580) note should be taken, aside from the various marchesi and dukes, of *Geometry* and *Architecture*, which once accompanied the paintings of the *Fasti gonzagheschi*, originally planned for here and painted by Tintoretto (1518-1594), now in Munich.

The following rooms follow iconographic programs apparently laid down by Pirro Ligorio, who was in the Palace in 1573.

In the Loggetta del Tasso (according to tradition Torquato Tasso lived in this small apartment between 1586 and 1587) the stucco reliefs are particularly interesting.

They depict the *History of Human Evolution*, as narrated by the Latin author Vitruvius in his *De Architectura* and by the Latin poet, Lucretius in his *De Natura Rerum*. Examples are the *Invention of Fire*, *Hunt*, *War* and, above all the *Inspirational Muses* of Art, also shown with the *Virtues* in the room of the Virtues (Sala delle Virtù) nearby (the cycles seem to have been executed by Lorenzo Costa the Younger).

Scalone di Enea (Staircase of Aeneas)

The Scalone di Enea, designed by Giovan Battista Bertani, leads to the Castle of San Giorgio, joined to the previous nucleus by a covered passageway, also by Bertani, while Giulio Romano had previously simply planned an aerial passageway closed by *"gelosie"* (shutters).

Above: *Castle of San Giorgio (15th cent.).*

Left: *the castle moat.*

Pages 38-39: *view of the Castle.*

Castle of San Giorgio

This impressive manor was built between 1390 and 1406 by the engineer Bartolino da Novara, who had also drawn up the first plan for the church of Santa Maria delle Grazie outside the city. His works in other Italian states include the Estense Castle in Ferrara, of 1385. The Castle of San Giorgio is an important part of the panorama of the city of Mantua, located in a peripheral site overlooking the lakes but also right next to the Gonzaga residence, surrounded by a moat and drawbridges. As the power of the Marchesi increased, it soon became an annex of their residence, and by the middle of the fifteenth century a series of artistically important works began to be added to the defensive structures and rooms. These included the rebuilding of the central court by Mantegna and Luca Fancelli and the Camera degli Sposi by Andrea Mantegna. In the sixteenth century the Castle and the Palace were almost merged and the basic structure of the Castle, originally composed of a central body and four imposing projecting corner towers, was concealed by a series of attached buildings. This nucleus was once more isolated in the course of the nineteenth-century restoration.

Right: *Castle courtyard.*

Below: *detail of the construction of the "opus affictum expeditum" upright according to Leon Battista Alberti.*

Courtyard of the Castle of San Giorgio

The court surrounded on three sides by porticoes is located at the center of the Castle. The north portico is late Gothic and dates to the early fifteenth century, while the other two were added, from 1472 on, by Luca Fancelli, following a design attributed to Andrea Mantegna. Although apparently there are no particular formal innovations in the structuring of the fifteenth-century wings with traditional arches springing from columns, the design of this complex, unfinished, is of great interest in the way in which the problem of the free corner column, which all by itself supports two porticoes set at right angles to each

other (a problem that fifteenth-century artists were particularly interested in), is treated. The solution offered here was that of introducing a pier at the center and another pier at each end. This anticipates the solution later adopted in the famous Courtyard of the Ducal Palace of Urbino (where Luciana Laurana, who had previously been in Mantua, worked after 1465). In Urbino the columns are transformed into half columns set against a corner pylon, while in the Courtyard of San Giorgio the columns remain autonomous, but are set very close to the pier. This is a highly antiquarian architectural construction, called "*affictum expeditum*" order by Leon Battista Alberti in his treatise, and the inevitable conclusion here is that Alberti had offered suggestions.

The upper floor is reached by means of a spiral ramp, also suitable for horses, and which calls to mind similar ramps in the towers of the Palace of Federico di Montefeltro in Urbino (an analogy due not only to the passage of Laurana from Mantua to Urbino, but also Alberti's friendship with both Ludovico Gonzaga and Federico da Montefeltro).

Camera degli Sposi or "Camera Picta"

Passing through the Sala del Fregio (of interest two small fifteenth-century panels with *St. Benedict* and *St. Scolastica*) and the Camera degli Stemmi, one reaches the Camera degli Sposi, known in the times of the Gonzaga as the "Camera Picta" or "Painted Room". This is one of the most celebrated rooms in all of Renaissance painting, and was painted between 1465 and 1474 by Andrea Mantegna for Ludovico and his wife Barbara of Brandenburg. As time passed it became a model for generations of artists, both for the beauty of the painting and for the scenic and per-

Camera degli Sposi by A. Mantegna.
Left: Città Antica *(detail).*

Below: The Encounter *(detail).*

Pages 42-43: *The Camera degli Sposi.*

spective innovations. For the occasion the room was architecturally modified by constructing a complex depressed barrel vault on lunettes and groins springing from small brackets at the sides (sort of wall capitals from which the stucco arches which decorate the ceiling spring). This construction seems to indicate that someone rather highly qualified was consulted (Leon Battista Alberti, who lived in Mantua between 1459 and 1460, had just been commissioned by Ludovico to design the church of San Sebastiano).

The picture probably refers to an episode in Gonzaga history dating to 1462 when Bianca Maria Visconti sent a message to the court in Mantua requesting them to hurry to Milan on account of the declining health of the duke, Francesco Sforza; another interpretation however is that the nomination to Cardinal of his son Francesco is being communicated to the marchese.

In any case it is Mantegna's only large decorative complex still in place and more or less as it was originally painted, despite numerous restorations. The room is practically cubical, not very large and with two windows. It was originally a bedroom, and on the south wall and the ceiling the iron hooks which supported the canopy are still in place. The room was certainly not a space used solely for study and therefore part of the private sphere, but also served as an Audience Hall for the more intimate members of the court and was where more reserved business was dealt with. In his decoration, Mantegna aimed at an illusionistic depiction of space, beginning with the

wreaths, antique urns. It has been suggested that this complex design represents a specific type of ancient architecture (perhaps the Roman *domus* or a sort of sun temple), studied in those years by Alberti in his treatise on architecture.

The two walls in shadow have been painted with damascened leather hangings, and the other two, lit by the raking light from the windows, are of outstanding beauty. On the west wall a series of pilasters, richly decorated in their candelabrum shafts, divide the painted space into three panels in which Mantegna has clearly diversified the perspective depth of the scenes. The figures in the foreground are set in very narrow spaces, painted to be seen from below. Their mass has therefore been considerably increased for the natural perspective viewpoint of the visitor, while the composition was planned by Mantegna on the basis of a clear-cut amplification of these volumes and through the contraposition of large masses. The luminous landscapes in the background also reveal these apparently anti-perspective studies: on the west wall, known as the wall of the Encounter, the ancient buildings are out of scale, with regards to their real distance, but their size and formal importance has been accentuated so that they will be clearly seen by the spectator, as revealed, for example, by the statue on the large altar in the panel on the right, which must be interpreted as a real colossus, on the basis of studies regarding vision but which is not based on those mathematical assumptions adopted, for example, so skilfully by Piero della Francesca. Mantegna takes an alternative route (and this is why these representations were so successful) not in opposition to the direction followed by Renaissance perspective, but on the contrary turning it into a study of the same mechanisms, but from a different point of view. These studies were then to result, in the sixteenth century and later, in a whole series of solutions in pictorial representations which were not only rigidly "mathematical" but also tonal.

famous open oculus in the center, where, under a marvelous blue sky with clouds, putti, animals, ladies and exotic figures look down over a balustrade (the balustrade, in addition to framing the sky, or a dome called in turn "Sky", is a motif very dear to Renaissance artists and is also found in the Church of S. Maria delle Carceri in Prato, after 1480). But there are any number of carefully worked out simulated effects, present in practically all the ornamentation in which a series of "tricks" meant to deceive the eye are used. On the ceiling it is not only the oculus which is illusionistically open, but also the garlands on the ribbing, supported by sham piers, are painted from the point of view of the spectator down below, while a series of eight rhomboid coffers form a sort of large rib framework, which actually serves no true architectural purpose. Set into this framework with lunettes are mythological scenes in the groins, eight medallions with Roman emperors, festooned garlands and

The scene on the wall, with a door in the center, takes place outside. In the foreground, on the right, close to the pier and the door, is *Ludovico Gonzaga* with his son *Cardinal Francesco*, while the figures talking together on the far right, are *King Christian I of Denmark*, the *Emperor Frederick III*, *Prince Frederico*, future marquis of Mantua. On the left are courtiers, as well as *dogs and horses*, animals particularly dear to the Gonzaga court. Over the door is the dedicatory inscription of this work, defined by Mantegna himself as "*tenue*" (light or soft).

This inscription is supported by graceful putti which echo their playful counterparts looking out over the balustrade above in the oculus, sticking their small heads through the railing. It has been suggested that the figure behind Ludovico is a *self-portrait* of the artist.

On the north wall, above the mantelpiece, is *Ludovico Gonzaga* with his wife *Barbara* (with near her a *Dwarf*) surrounded by members of the family and court, who are discussing the contents of the letter. Against a background of blue skies with clouds and garlands of fruit, a beautiful curtain with a pattern of golden racemes is drawn to one side to reveal a marble shrine with polychrome inlays behind the seated figures of the Marchese and Marchesa. Along the roof are antiquarian decorations (antefixes),

Preceding page, above and below: Dogs, Horses and Pages, (details).

Above: The Gonzaga dogs (detail).

Pages 46-47: Ludovico II and Barbara of Brandenburg.

resembling those Leon Battista Alberti set on the Tempietto in the Rucellai Chapel in Florence. This clearly demonstrates how the relationship between Mantegna and Alberti was marked by a lively exchange of ideas.

This page:
Gentlemen of
the court
*(detail).
Mantegna's
method of
perspective
structure was
not particularly
appreciated in
the sixteenth
century by the
Classical trend
of Raphael's
Roman school,
as evidenced by
the description
of this room by
Sebastiano
Serlio, who
criticized the
crowding of the
figures.*

Facing page:
*ceiling, the
perspective
trompe l'oeil.*

Preceding page, above: *putti holding a cartouche*; below, left to right: *decorative* *detail of a frieze; candelabra with the supposed Self-portrait of Mantegna.* Above: *some of Ludovico II's children (detail).*

then by Bertani. Through the Sala delle Conchiglie (or Cappe), with late sixteenth-century marine decorations and grotesques, a descending ramp leads to the *Grotta di Isabella*, a fine studiolo created between 1490 when the Marchesa entered the city, and 1507. To be noted is the lovely gilded wooden ceiling with Isabella's heraldic devices, executed between 1506 and 1508.

Then back up to the Sala delle Armi, so-called because of the heraldic arms painted on the walls by Giulio Romano in 1531, which communicates with the private Chapel which Bertani created for Guglielmo from a pre-existent room (hence the asymmetrical plan).

The Gabinetti della Paleologa or the Palazzina di Margherita Paleologa
(Cabinets or Small Palace of Margherita Paleologa)

Adjacent to Bertani's chapel are the so-called Gabinetti della Paleologa, small rooms which contain what remains of the highly interesting Palazzina built by Giulio Romano in 1531 and torn down in 1829 in the nineteenth-century restoration of the presumed medieval aspect of the castle.

Commissioned from Giulio Romano as an addition to the Castle on the occasion of the marriage of Margherita Paleologa del Monferrato with Federico Gonzaga, the building was a sort of small villa connected to the ducal apartments, with a private garden and a loggia, perhaps somewhat like the Appartamento di Troia nearby.

The rooms inside were then frescoed with putti, Gonzaga coats of arms and grotesques by Giulio Romano and his school from 1532 on, partially documented by nineteenth-century photographs. A covered bridge joined it to the castle. The palazzina was of particular interest because it was the only example of a building with a superposition of architectural orders (here treated as simple Tuscan pilaster strips), after the creation of the facade of the *Domus Nova* by Luca Fancelli overlooking the lake (also unfinished).

Still to be seen is the *Gabinetto degli Armadi* with a ceiling frescoed by Andreasino with *putti*, after which comes the *Gabinetto delle Sibille* of the second half of the sixteenth century and then the *Gabinetto delle Stagioni* by a pupil of Giulio Romano.

The *Scaletta dei Martiri* leads to the upper floors, with rooms used in the nineteenth century as a political prison where Tito Speri and Pietro Frattini (nineteenth-century Lombard patriots) were imprisoned.

Of note here is the sixteenth-century *Stanza dello Zodiaco*.

Apartment of Duke Ludovico II and of Isabella d'Este

Next come the suite of rooms renovated by Ludovico II (who ruled from 1444 to 1478) to serve as residence for himself and his wife Barbara of Brandenburg. The beginning of this radical transformation of the Castle took place in 1459. Isabella d'Este, wife of Francesco II (lord of the city from 1484 to 1519) later also lived here until 1523 when she had a new apartment installed in the "Corte Vecchia".

Entrance is through the Sala dei Soli (after the suns which decorate the ceiling), where the fine mantelpiece, in the style of Fancelli and Mantegna, is all that remains of its fifteenth-century aspect, for the room was later transformed by Giulio Romano and

Nuovo Appartamento di Isabella d'Este in "Corte Vecchia"
(New Apartment of Isabella d'Este in the "New Court")

The entrance to the apartment to which the Marchesa had her furnishings and studiolo transferred in 1519 is reached by retracing one's steps through Bertani's Corridor, which joins the Castle and the Corte Nuova to the Corte Vecchia, and returning to the ground floor. The rooms are arranged around the Secret Garden, finished in 1522, rectangular in plan and surrounded by a high wall, with free or attached columns, with niches in between (which contained statues) on the north. The Latin inscription in the frieze reads "fece Isabelle Estense, nipote dei Re d'Aragona, figlia e sorella dei Duchi di Ferrara, sposa e madre dei Duchi di Mantova nell'anno 1522 dalla nascita di Cristo". (made for Isabelle Estense, descended from the Kings of Aragon, daughter and sister of the Dukes of Ferrara, bride and mother of the Dukes of Mantua in the year 1522 after the birth of Christ). Water plays and frescoes completed this small private court with Ionic columns supporting an entablature and set on canonical Vitruvian bases. This architectural decoration had generally been attributed to Giovan Battista Bertani, who was particularly interested in the Ionic order, but the discovery of the inscription in the frieze with the date "1522" would seem to indicate that it was designed before the arrival of Giulio Romano in Mantua by Giovan Battista Covo. This artist played an important role in the Gonzaga court and was later an assistant to Giulio in St. Peter's and is known to have been involved in the work in this wing of the palace (but the question remains of whether the Covo always mentioned in the documents as "capomastro" or master builder would really have been capable of creating this Ionic order, whose beauty was so difficult and obscure that years later Bertani wrote a treatise on this subject alone). The inscription, on the other hand, may have been set there after "1522", since whoever designed these columns which compare to the studies Bertani set on his own house (see pp. 85-86) had to be well acquainted with architectural theory.

Sala della Scalcheria or of Leonbruno
(Room of the Scalcheria or of Leonbruno)

The Room, known also as *Camera Grande* or *Scalcheria* (room for carving meat), is decorated with scenes of the hunt executed between 1520 and 1523 by Lorenzo Leonbruno. Landscapes are also painted in the lunettes, while medallions and grotesques surround the tondo at the center of the ceiling, where the figures looking down at the observer were clearly inspired by

Courtyard of the Appartamento Nuovo of   *Isabella, Ionic columns (details).*

Mantegna's Camera degli Sposi. An antique bust of *Faustina* (n.6749) kept here, said to have belonged to Mantegna and later bought by Isabella, is now considered a "rather mediocre piece" and hardly worth the high price we know the Marchesa paid to the painter.

Lo Studiolo

This small private room, typical of the humanist courts, with a fine carved and gilded wooden ceiling, was made together with the adjacent Grotta (restored in 1933). The wainscoting is articulated by small flattened columns with a decorated shaft, typically fifteenth-century. Paintings by Mantegna, Lorenzo Costa the Elder, Perugino, now all in the Louvre, were set in the spaces between the columns. The majolica floor was a perfect finishing touch to this extremely elegant room (a few tiles are on exhibit in a case in the adjacent Corridor). As furnishings the Marchesa brought in small marble tables, ivory chairs, objects in alabaster, and antique sculpture.

La Grotta (The Grotta)

Entrance to the so-called Grotta, extremely refined in taste, is through a marble doorway carved by Giancristoforo Romano or perhaps Tullio Lombardo (with fine tondos). The room was modeled on the Grotto previously built for the Marchesa in the Castle of San Giorgio, with its coffered barrel vault raised like a pavilion and in particular the wainscoting with its marquetry of architectural views, Isabella's heraldic devices, musical instruments, as

well as the notes of the song "*prenez sur moi*" (press on me) and the motto "*nec spe nec metu*" (neither hope nor fear) accompanied by various symbols such as the number XVII, alpha and omega, playing cards, the candlestick with an unlit candle. These panels were made in 1506 by the Mola brothers: only six of those there now are original and two of these show fifteenth-century city landscapes with genre scenes (fishermen, boatmen). The carenated ceiling in gold and blue dates to 1522. Around 1600 rare and precious antique objects from the Marchesa's private collection were kept in the cupboards and niches, closed by the wall panels.

After finishing the museum itinerary of the Ducal Palace, access can be gained to the rooms located between the Corte Vecchia and the Castle of San Giorgio which are still part of the Gonzaga complex, by crossing Piazza Sordello towards the lake and entering the Prato del Castello through Bertani's Arch.

Appartamento Nuovo of Isabella. Left, above: *ceiling of the Studiolo.*

Below, left to right: *entrance doorway to the Grotto and detail.*

L'Arco del Bertani and Il Prato del Castello (Piazza Castello)
(Bertani's Arch and Piazza Castello)

In 1549, Giovan Battista Bertani set up a large triumphal arch as the entrance to the Palace from the courtyard known as Prato del Castello. The arch was originally an ephemeral urban decoration for the visit to the city of Philip of Hapsburg (future king of Spain as Philip II).

The structure was so successful that the architect was nominated permanent superintendent of the ducal construction yards, and a representation of the arch was even sent to Tintoretto in Venice so he could include it in one of his paintings, now in Munich, of the *Fasti gonzagheschi*, or *Gonzaga Court Celebrations*, for the visit to Mantua of the Hapsburg sovereign. The duke subsequently had the architect build the arch in masonry as the entrance to the Palace, on the side of the Lungolago, at the same time charging him with qualifying the large Prato del Castello. After Giulio Romano's additions to the Palace on the side of the Lago Inferiore, the remaining area consisted of a sort of wedge-shaped space between the Corte Vecchia and the Castello.

Bertani was requested to provide it with a precise architectural personality by adding four arcaded porticoes, articulated by a Serlian motif (that is with columns supporting a portion of entablature from which the arch springs), which worked together to create a highly scenographic backdrop, without any visual fulcrum. The exedra which now creates a break in the wing adjacent to the Castle was added for Duke Vincenzo by the architect Viani in the early seventeenth century when tendencies were oriented towards a quest for a visual point, for a salient pause in the fluid movement of the arches.

Above:
Bertani's Arch.

Right: *Piazza Castello.*

Facing page:
Palatine Basilica of S. Barbara (1575 and after 1587).

Archive data list 1595 as the date on which work on the right wing, where the old Cancelleria was housed, was begun. The external wing, on the south, contains Bertani's Corridor, which we know was begun in 1581, while the building on the north had housed the Teatro di Corte since 1549 (first by Bertani, then in 1588 by Ippolito Andreasi, then rebuilt in 1706 by Ferdinando Galli Bibiena and in 1783 by Luigi Piermarini. In 1898 it was definitively torn down). The dating of the present structures, in other words, is anything but clear.

By passing under Bertani's Corridor (or Corridor of Santa Barbara) one reaches Piazza Santa Barbara, a small square systematized in 1582 by Bernardino Faciotto and then again in 1780 by Paolo Pozzo, where the Basilica of Santa Barbara stands.

Palatine Basilica of Santa Barbara

In the middle of the sixteenth century work was in progress on various chapels for the ducal palace and mention is made of the completion of the chapel next to the duke's apartment in the Castle of San Giorgio in July 1561, by Bertani (Bertani's Chapel). A few months later work was begun on the much more demanding complex of Santa Barbara, to serve as the palatine church where services were to be held for court ceremonies involving personages of high rank.

At the time the small church of Santa Croce, various buildings including houses, and spaces used for playing ball, a popular game in the courts of the second half of the sixteenth century, stood on this site. The first construction phase of the basilica of Santa Barbara, marked by periods of tension between Guglielmo and the architect, ended with the erection of the bell tower in 1567, while the second phase began in 1569 and aimed at lengthening the church that had already been built in a Greek-cross plan, which at this point contrasted with the new dispositions of the Council of Trent requiring long churches.

Entrance is through an elegant pronaos (porch) with three arches and pilaster strips, a rhythmical articulation which continues on either side of the porch, thus creating a sort of unbroken horizontal facade. On the left, detached, but incorporated in the "portico", is the bell tower with a sort of round aedicule at the top.

The fact that the bell tower is detached from the body of the church, has led to the hypothesis that Bertani may have taken inspiration from San Biagio in Montepulciano by Antonio da Sangallo the Elder and that a twin tower may originally have been planned on the left of the basilica in Mantua.

The curious interior is the result of the addition of a raised sanctuary, closed by eighteenth-century railing. This addition, in line with precepts of the Counter Reformation, completely overturned the spatial composition of the original church with its four symmetrical sides and large central dome. Another dome was set over the high altar at the back of the church, where the catafalques for the funerals of the Dukes were also placed. Over the side altars, dating to around 1572, are works by Mantuan artists, in particular Lorenzo Costa the Younger, including the *Baptism of Constantine* on the right and the *Martyrdom of Saint Hadrian* on the left.

To be noted over the lesser altars are the *St. Peter Receiving the Keys* by Luigi Costa and the *Magdalen* by Andreasino, while the *Martyrdom of Saint Barbara*, by Domenico Brusasorci (1516-1567) is in the apse.

The wing built to house the rectory of Santa Barbara can almost certainly also be attributed to Bertani (originally two other additional wings were included in the project) and dated to 1575, even though it was built by Pompeo Pedemonte, after the plague which struck Mantua in 1587.

- Cathedral of San Pietro
- Rigoletto's House
- Tower of the Cage and Palazzo Acerbi (or Guerrieri)
- Palazzo Castiglioni or Bonacolsi
- Palazzo degli Uberti
- Bishop's Palace or Palazzo Bianchi
- Voltone (Archway) of San Pietro
- Accademia Virgiliana
- Teatro Scientifico
- Palazzo degli Studi and State Archives
- Church of SS. Trinità
- Arch of the Arengario and Palazzo del Massaro
- Palazzo del Podestà or Palazzo del Broletto
- Piazza delle Erbe
- Palazzo della Ragione and Clock Tower
- Rotonda of San Lorenzo
- House of Giovanni Boniforte da Concorezzo
- Basilica of Sant'Andrea
- Piazza Marconi
- Loggia dei Mercanti and Palazzo della Camera di Commercio
- former Jewish Ghetto

- Rabbi's palace
- Palazzo Sordi
- Palazzo della Finanza
- Church of San Martino
- The Rio
- House of Giovan Battista Bertani
- Norsa Synagogue
- Church of Santa Maria della Carità
- Pescherie (Fish Market)

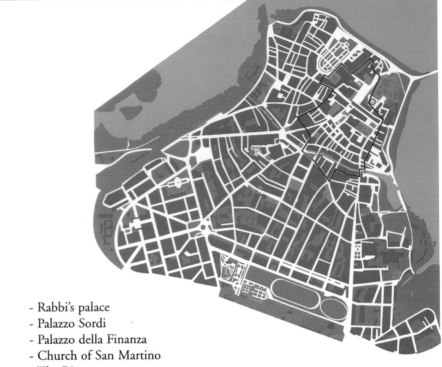

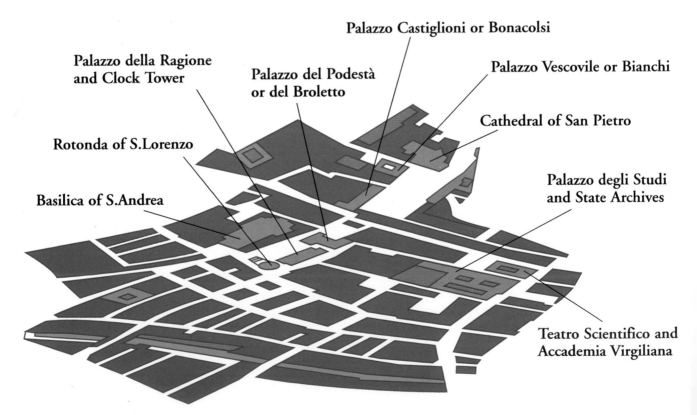

Palazzo Castiglioni or Bonacolsi

Palazzo della Ragione and Clock Tower

Palazzo del Podestà or del Broletto

Palazzo Vescovile or Bianchi

Rotonda of S.Lorenzo

Cathedral of San Pietro

Palazzo degli Studi and State Archives

Basilica of S.Andrea

Teatro Scientifico and Accademia Virgiliana

DUOMO OR CATHEDRAL OF SAN PIETRO

In 1549 Giovan Battista Bertani was nominated "Soprintendente alle Fabbriche Ducali" for the reconstruction of the Cathedral of Mantua. The work had already been planned and begun by Giulio Romano (assisted by the *capomastro* Battista Covo), who died before the work was finished. He had however left a wooden model. Bertani's task, which he himself said was extremely demanding, was addressed primarily to the completion of the transept and choir, the installation of supporting piers for the choir stalls based on ancient columns seen by the architect in Rome and the construction, in 1551, of a new facade, never finished, to replace the late Gothic facade designed by the Dalle Masegne. Gerolamo Genga, called to the Gonzaga court in 1548, had also proposed various changes. Bertani may have gone ahead on his own without following Giulio Romano's model, especially in the dome and in the supporting piers.

The present facade in Carrara marble was built between 1756 and 1761 by the Roman architect Nicolò Baschiera in a style which combined the Neoclassic purism then coming into fashion with the Mannerist models of the latter half of the sixteenth century and the Baroque. While the main part of the facade is articulated by a giant order of Corinthian pilasters, the large triangular pediment at the top, which is unrelated to the actual height of the building, is typically Mannerist in the way it makes the central portion project forward. The strongly projecting upper part also helps creates an effect that is actually Baroque. The front elevations of the side aisles, with straight walls and statues above (by Giovanni Angelo Finali and Giuseppe Tivani, present from 1752 to 1756) clearly refer both to classical examples and the great works of Roman Baroque Classicism. The flank elevation is quite unlike that of the main

Below:
Cathedral of San Pietro (the facade dates to 1756).

Cathedral of San Pietro, detail of the lateral gables.

facade with triangular cusp terminations which recall the late Gothic style of the Venetians Pierpaolo and Iacobello Dalle Masegne, who worked on the facade between 1395 and 1401. The famous painting in the Ducal Palace of the *Expulsion of the Bonacolsi by the Gonzaga*, signed and dated 1494, by Domenico Morone, shows us what the cathedral looked like before it was remodeled in the sixteenth century. The present cusped terminations are however more of a nineteenth-century interpretation than authentic medieval elements.

The Cathedral already existed in the eleventh century and was rebuilt more than once. Walls of the Gothic chapels still remain on the right flank while the bell tower is Romanesque. The interior was completely renewed after a tremendous fire in 1545, to a design by Giulio Romano, who however died the following year, and then by Bertani. A large dome on an octagonal drum stands over the sanctuary of the five-aisled Latin-cross basilica. In line with Giulio Romano's concept of the antique and modelled on the early Christian basilica, the nave is higher than the side-aisles from which it is separated by magnificent Corinthian columns supporting an entablature. The nave has a coffered ceiling while the adjacent aisles have antique Roman barrel vaults. The outer aisles once more have a flat ceiling, a sort of theme and variation recalling the early Christian basilicas of Rome. The chapels along the side walls were systematized by Bertani and Antonio Maria Viani and contain various works of note. In the first chapel on the

right is a painting with the *Miracle of Saint Egidio* by the school of Guercini dating to the seventeenth century, while an elegant eighteenth-century railing is at the entrance. A fine early Christian sarcophagus dating to the fourth-fifth century, set against the outer wall, was already in Mantua in the early sixteenth century. A marble fourteenth-century altar frontal and a seventeenth-century altarpiece with the *Crucifixion* are in the second chapel. The fourth chapel, or Baptistery, set into the base of the campanile, has traces of fourteenth-century frescoes and a *Crucifixion* as well as figures of the *Evangelists*. There are a series of frescoes done between the late sixteenth and early seventeenth century in the right arm of the transept. They are by Ippolito Andreasi known as Andreasino and Teodoro Ghisi, and depict the *Council of Mantua in 1459* and various worshipping personages on the ceiling. Late sixteenth-century altarpieces are over the altars.

The dome fresco of the *Glory of Paradise* is by Andreasino, while there are two sixteenth-century canvases in the choir. Next to the altar, on the left, is the *Vision of Saint John Evangelist* by Gerolamo Mazzola Bedoli (1500-1569), while the fresco in the apse conch of the *Apotheosis of the Redemption* generally thought to be by Domenico Fetti has recently been attributed to Antonio Maria Viani. At the end of the left arm of the transept, with other frescoes by Andreasino and Ghisi as well as eighteenth-century paintings by Felice Campi, is the entrance to the Chapel of the Sacrament. It dates to the second half of the seventeenth century and was designed by Alfonso Moscatelli, who used Viani's church of Sant'Orsola as model. This room, with an octagonal ground plan, is covered by a dome and was decorated by Felice Campi and Leandro Marconi in 1784 on the basis of an iconographic program prepared by Paolo Pozzo, with the addition of finely sculptured columns, pilasters and stone arches, attributed to Pietro and Tullio Lombardo who were active between the fifteenth and sixteenth centuries (the relief of *Philoctetes* in the Appartamento di Guastalla in the Ducal Palace is also ascribed to them). Two of the paintings on the walls were mentioned by Vasari as works by sixteenth-century Veronese artists: *Saint Margaret* by Domenico Brusasorci and *Saint Martin*, by Paolo Farinati. A doorway in the left aisle opens onto the corridor that leads to the Cappella dell'Incoronata (or dei Voti) dating to about 1480, commissioned by Ludovico II Gonzaga and probably designed by Luca Fancelli. Together with the adjacent sacristy, it was to have been a single T-shaped room, which was very Florentine in style, before the changes of the last century when various smaller rooms were

Above and below: *interior of the* *Cathedral of San Pietro.*

Giulio Romano and a canvas with the *Magdalen* by Battista del Moro, an artist mentioned by Vasari, together with Fermo Ghisoni.

In the left side-aisle, in the third chapel, is an altarpiece with *Saint Lucy* by Ghisoni, while in the second is a canvas with *Saint Speciosa* by Gerolamo Mazzola Bedoli. Sixteenth-century stucco statues of the school of Giulio Romano set between one chapel and the next complete the decoration of this part.

CASA DEL RIGOLETTO
(Rigoletto's House)

There is a house behind the cathedral, belonging to the Canons, where Rigoletto, on whom Verdi based his opera and to whom the statue in the courtyard refers, is said to have lived.

TORRE DELLA GABBIA and PALAZZO ACERBI (or GUERRIERI)
(Tower of the Cage and Palazzo Acerbi)

created. The frescoes on the walls are by Andreasino and Ghisi.

The adjacent Sacristy, initially part of the larger chapel, has vine tendrils and medallions of the school of Mantegna referring to the *Mysteries of the Virgin* on the ceiling. On the walls are frescoes of the school of

The Torre della Gabbia in Via Cavour, dating to the fourteenth century and over fifty meters high, rises up over the rooftops on the southern side of Piazza Sordello. It has been repeatedly restored. In 1576 an iron cage, in which criminals were displayed to the public, was installed about halfway up. This

Above:
Martyrdom of
Saint Agatha,
*by Lorenzo
Costa.*

Right:
*courtyard of
Rigoletto's
House.*

Torre della Gabbia (14th cent.) and Palazzo Acerbi; in the background, the dome of the basilica of S. Andrea.

idea appealed to the collective fantasy, in particular the typical nineteenth-century taste for a certain grim past, and the cage has been put back where it was in the sixteenth century.

The medieval Palazzo Acerbi (or Guerrieri) stands in the southern corner of the Piazza Sordello between the Torre della Gabbia and the Voltone di San Pietro. The battlements with their merlons, like those of the adjacent palaces, were the result of nineteenth-centu-ry restoration which attempted to restore its presumed medieval look to the piazza.

The palazzo also overlooks Via Cavour with an addition dating to the sixteenth century, while there are traces of fourteenth-century frescoes in the courtyard which was renovated in the Renaissance. The family chapel, frescoed in the fourteenth century, was of interest, but it was dismantled in the course of the nineteenth century.

PALAZZO CASTIGLIONI

The building, traditionally thought to have belonged to the Bonacolsi, was probably built by the Gonzaga and was heavily restored in the nineteenth century. To be noted is the Renaissance portal at no. 12, from the monastery of San Giovanni and with the heraldic devices of Isabella d'Este in the decorated pilaster strips, consisting of the alpha and omega joined together and the triangular candlestick with a

Right: *Torre della Gabbia (Tower of the Cage).*

Far right, above: *detail of the Cage.*

Below: *facade of the Palazzo Castiglioni or Bonacolsi.*

single candle. These devices also appear in her apartments in the Ducal Palace.

PALAZZO DEGLI UBERTI

The Palazzo degli Uberti was built by the exiled Florentine Uberti family. Remains of the original one-light openings and cornices can still be identified, as well as a few traces of fifteenth-century frescoes, above all on the first floor

PALAZZO VESCOVILE or PALAZZO BIANCHI (Bishop's Palace or Palazzo Bianchi)

Built between 1776 and 1786 as the palace for the Marchesi Bianchi, it passed to the Curia in 1823. In its austere Neoclassic style, the facade is distinguished

Left: *facade of Palazzo Bianchi.*
Below: *Voltone or Archway of San Pietro.*

by the two telamon figures (Atlas figures) which frame the entrance, as in many patrician Viennese palaces, as well as by the balustrade above, which is classically crowned by statues.

The City Center

Around 1190 the new city center was built in the area that up till the twelfth century had been located outside the city walls and consisted of fields and vegetable gardens. The waters of the river Mincio were deviated to provide a defensive structure, with the formation of the four lakes (now *Lago Inferiore*, di *Mezzo* and *Superiore*, as well as the Lago Paiolo on the south which has been drained). Mantua was thus turned into a large river island defended on all four sides by lakes and fortifications.

VOLTONE DI SAN PIETRO (Archway)

In Antiquity and in the early Middle Ages the city limits (*Civitas vetus*) were marked by what is now Via Accademia, on the other side of the Voltone di San Pietro. Access was through a city gate, which in the subsequent urban expansion of 1190 was transformed into the Voltone di San Pietro.

The passageway was then once more rebuilt in the sixteenth century, probably by the architect Giovan Battista Bertani, to mark the passage from Piazza Sordello, of specifically "Gonzaga" pertinence, to the centers of city life.

Further on are the main piazzas of Mantua (note the fine capitals on the portico on the right).

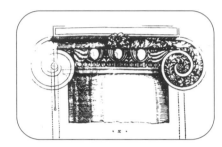

(Via Accademia - Piazza Dante)
ACCADEMIA VIRGILIANA

The building which now houses the Accademia Nazionale Virgiliana was built by Giuseppe Piermarini (1734-1808) between 1771 and 1775 for the empress Maria Theresa of Hapsburg. The architect paid particular attention to the design of the Neoclassic monumental facade on Via dell'Accademia, using a giant order of Ionic pilasters (shallow engaged pilasters which rise without a break from the ground level almost to the roof) supporting an entablature with an inscription in the frieze (which however dates to 1891) and a generous crowning above.

In this sense the structure is an outstanding example of the cultural updating of the new idioms of Milanese Neoclassicism, introduced into Mantua by an architect of such high standing as Giuseppe Piermarini and is one of the finest examples of the building activity, both public and private, which flourished in the first period of Austrian rule (1707-1797).

An attempt was being made at this time to restore its original splendor to the city, as one of the Italian strongholds of culture and of Viennese good government, after the previous vicissitudes involving the Gonzaga and the wars of succession.

Above: *Ionic capital in the portico in Via Broletto, based on an example by Bertani.*

Right: *depiction of an Ionic Capital from:* G.B. Bertani, Gli oscuri et difficili passi dell'opera ionica, *Mantua, 1556.*

Below: *facade of the Accademia Virgiliana.*

AERE   CIVITATIS   PERFECTVM   ANNO   MDCCCLXXXXI

TEATRO SCIENTIFICO

The Accademia building, dating in its general layout more or less to the sixteenth century when the "Accademia degli Invaghiti" was founded, houses an interesting academic library (containing works by Virgil), but also the Teatro Scientifico, an outstanding example of Baroque theater architecture. It was built between 1767 and 1769 by Antonio Galli Bibiena (1700-1774) and then incorporated when the entire complex was renovated by Giuseppe Piermarini. The inside consists of an unusual bell-shaped space, with four tiers of boxes and a fixed stage set with monochrome chiaroscuro wall paneling by Bibiena with pastoral scenes.

On the upper floor is a rectangular room by Paolo Pozzo from Verona (1741-1803), with stuccowork and paintings of the Austrian sovereigns, of 1770.

In 1769 the young Mozart played in this theater. To be noted, in the distance on the right, the Torre degli Zuccari, an example of a medieval patrician tower house.

Above: *facade of the Teatro Scientifico;* below: *interior.*

(Via Ardigò-Largo Luigi Gonzaga)

PALAZZO DEGLI STUDI and ARCHIVIO DI STATO

In 1620 the Jesuit Order began building the Palazzo degli Studi as the seat of its civic university. In 1763, on the project of the Bolognese architect Alfonso Torregiani (1682-1764), who also designed Palazzo Cavriani, the facade was re-adapted to emphasize the great entrance portal, flanked by pilasters and with a large semi-circular pediment with an elegant coat of arms at the center. A bit further on is the complex which houses the State Archives, a solemn example of eighteenth- and nineteenth-century neomedieval renovation, in particular the tower and the "Romanesque" two-light windows in the facade.

CHURCH OF SS. TRINITA'

In 1597 a parcel of land occupied in the second half of the sixteenth century by the Jesuit order which had recently come to the city, became the site of the church of the Trinità. The building, preceded by a small *sagrato* or church square, is now used as a deposit by the neighboring State Archives. The facade was completely transformed in the nineteenth century when it was articulated in two orders topped by a classical pediment. In 1797 the French troops removed two famous canvases attributed to Rubens from the apse, while a third, damaged, depicting the *Gonzaga Family in Adoration of the Holy Trinity* is now on view in the Ducal Palace in Mantua.

(Piazza Broletto)

ARCO DELL'ARENGARIO and PALAZZO DEL MASSARO (Arengario Passageway and Palazzo del Massaro)

After passing the building which houses the Museo Tazio Nuvolari (a car-racing champion, born in Mantua, at n. 9 Piazza Broletto), the Voltone dell'Arengario presents itself to the visitor. The original layout dates to the early fourteenth century and it

was built to connect the Palazzo del Podestà with the Palazzo del Massaro where the administrator of the City's property resided. The arch, with a facade articulated by two three-light openings below and a gallery above, was greatly restored in the centuries and its present aspect is the result of heavy neo-Romantic reconstruction. Of particular interest are the frescoes dating to 1432-44 showing a *Perspective View of the City of Mantua*, located in the rooms on the ground floor of the Palazzo del Massaro; there are also rooms decorated with heraldic devices of Gianfrancesco Gonzaga.

PALAZZO DEL PODESTA' or PALAZZO DEL BROLETTO

Construction of the Palazzo del Podestà began in 1227, on commission of the then podestà of Mantua,

Loderengo Martinengo. It was subsequently damaged by fire in 1413 and then restored several times by the Gonzaga, until finally, after 1462, Luca Fancelli was called in. The building is composed of two contiguous structures, one overlooking the Piazza Broletto with the tall Town Tower (Torre Comunale), the other overlooking Piazza delle Erbe. There were originally two symmetrical towers on the second structure but the one on the southeast was torn down by Andreani in the early 1900s, leaving the tower facing out on the street. Restorations, in particular those in a neo-Romantic key, were aimed at unifying the facades by adding a crenellated crowning which was later filled in. The Mannerist marble facing on the lowest part of the Town Tower, dating to the second half of the sixteenth century, is attributed by some to Bertani, and seems to be the result of a desire to make the piazza look more modern. A porticoed passageway, known as dei Lattonai, leads to the courtyard, while near it, towards Piazza Broletto, is a modern copy, set in a medieval aedicule, of the thirteenth-century statue of the *Seated Virgil*, of which the original is in the Ducal Palace.

Piazza delle Erbe

A street originally laid out in the twelfth century and lined with porticoed houses (to be noted the Palazzo Andreasi, at n. 55-56, with a fine brick cornice of the late fifteenth century and the Casa della Stadera, where the public scales were, with remains of early sixteenth-century frescoes attributed to Pordenone) leads to the Piazza delle Erbe from the Piazza del Broletto. Many of these porticoes, some of them late Gothic, were built thanks to the initiatives of the dukes, Francesco I (1382-1407) and Gian Francesco Gonzaga (1407-1444).

The name of the piazza derives from the fact that as early as the Middle Ages this was where the fruit and vegetable market was held. It is a fine urban space surrounded by monuments of various periods, such as the Palazzo del Podestà (the principal facade is on Piazza Broletto), the Palazzo della Ragione with the Torre dell'Orologio, the Rotonda di San Lorenzo and the House of the Milanese merchant Boniforte with the Torre del Salaro.

PALAZZO DELLA RAGIONE and TORRE DELL'OROLOGIO (Palazzo della Ragione and Clock Tower)

The building, also known as "Palazzo Nuovo" since it was built in 1250 after the adjacent Palazzo del Podestà to which it is connected by a passageway, has a fifteenth-century portico originally occupied by shops. Its present general design is the result of modifications carried out by Luca Fancelli, who oriented the front of the building towards Piazza del Mercato, at the same time renovating various buildings in the square to give them greater uniformity. The upper floor, seat of the administration of justice in Gonzaga times as well, is articulated by seven large three-light windows, the result of restoration as is the crenellated crowning above. Inside, in correspondence to the row of three-light windows, is the great *salone*, typical of medieval public palaces, where traces of thirteenth-century frescoes are still visible. They show *Prophets* and the *Last Judgement*, the work of a painter who signed himself "Grixopoulos" from Parma. To the right of the palace stands the great Torre dell'Orologio, or Clock Tower, built in 1473 by Luca Fancelli, on the advice of Leon Battista Alberti. The large clock at the center was originally built by the mathematician Bartolomeo Manfredi (known as

Piazza delle Erbe; on the left, the dome of Sant'Andrea and on the right, the Palazzo del Podestà or del Broletto.

Palazzo della Ragione and Torre dell'Orologio.
Left, above: *fresco of the* Last Judgement *(13th cent.)* and below: Court Scenes *(13th cent.).*

Above: *Clock* *(16th and 19th cent.)*

Below: *facade of the Palace, detail.*

Bartolomeo dell'Orologio), with a mechanism that marked the months and the positions of the stars as well as the hours.

What we see today is the result of a nineteenth-century restoration, while below, in a niche, is an early seventeenth-century statue of the *Madonna Immacolata*.

The crowning of the Tower, by Antonio Maria Viani, dates to 1612.

ROTONDA OF SAN LORENZO

The Rotonda of San Lorenzo stands to the right of the Torre dell'Orologio, on a level lower than the square. This circular Romanesque church, which according to tradition is the oldest church in Mantua, built in 1082 for Matilda of Canossa, may actually date to the first half of the following century. In 1579 Guglielmo Gonzaga had the building closed to worship and partially torn down.

It was subsequently incorporated into the adjacent buildings. Not until 1908-1926 was the old building brought back to light and the missing parts were rebuilt in a neo-Romanesque interpretation.

The interior consists of a central core, whose taller roof is visible from the outside, surrounded by a two-storied ring aisle.

The upper part was the matroneum, supported on stumpy round masonry piers, which like the walls were originally plastered. Remains of twelfth- and thirteenth-century frescoes with *Christ as Judge*

Right: *Rotonda of San Lorenzo (1082 and then 1908-1926).*

Facing page: *view of the monumental center with the Rotonda of San Lorenzo, the Clock Tower and the Basilica of Sant'Andrea.*

and figures of *angels*, in Byzantine style, appear on the vault and to the left of the altar, marked by marble columns, while remains of early Christian interlaced pilaster strips and bunches of grapes are also still visible.

CASA DI GIOVAN BONIFORTE DA CONCOREZZO
(House of G. Boniforte da Concorezzo)

The residence of the wealthy merchant Boniforte da Concorezzo, who dealt in luxury goods, was built at one end of Piazza Mantegna, near the fourteenth-century Torre del Salaro, in 1455, as indicated by a triple inscription in Latin, Italian and Mantuan vernacular.

The building, adjoining an old salt tower, dominates the principal street of Mantua with a facade characterized by its symmetry. It was originally designed on four levels beginning with the portico at ground level to end with a covered roof-terrace at the top. The entablature was decorated with fine carvings illustrating the luxury merchandise in which Boniforte dealt, and in the materials and splendor of the decorations the residence vied with the neighboring public and private buildings.

In line with Leon Battista Alberti's dictates, a trabeated portico, as in the Boniforte house, was meant to be a distinctive formal characteristic for patrician dwellings with respect to the houses of the common citizens with their arches.

A few years after it was built, the house had already become a touchstone for the renewal of Mantuan architecture in line with humanist, in particular Albertian, canons, and was often mentioned in documents of the 1460s as a point of reference for topographical indications.

Piazza Mantegna
BASILICA OF SANT'ANDREA

The basilica of Sant'Andrea, the largest religious building in Mantua, is one of the best known Renaissance churches, and not only because it was designed by Leon Battista Alberti, but also because of the formal innovations in the plan. The origin of the complex is traditionally set in the ninth century, with the construction of a building to house the relic of the blood of Christ, brought to Mantua by Longinus, the soldier who had pierced the side of Christ on the cross with his lance, was then converted and had collected earth bathed with the blood of the Savior. When he reached Mantua, Longinus hid the jars containing this holy earth, and in 804, almost eight centuries later, they were discovered, and a sanctuary was built so these holy relics could be worshipped. In 1037 a Benedictine monastery was built next to the church, but in 1472 the abbey prelature was abolished by pope Sixtus IV, who set cardinal Francesco Gonzaga at the head of the new collegiate church. In that same year the complete renovation of the old building was begun by Luca Fancelli on a project by Alberti with the transformation of the original nucleus, of which the bell tower erected on the left in 1413 is still standing. In 1470 Alberti and Ludovico Gonzaga were already exchanging letters regarding a new church of which a model was sent to Mantua. The building, according to Alberti's dictates, was to be unusual ("*mirabile*"), large enough to hold great crowds and, above all, modeled on a heretofore unused type, that of the Etruscan temple. Problems set in immediately when the designer died in 1472, first regarding the foundations, then in relation to the restraints set by the neighboring buildings, and finally lack of money. In 1477 the crisis in the construction yard had reached the point where Fancelli had to let all his masons go, and by the end of 1485 he himself was no longer Superintendent of works. The vault over the nave was finished by 1494 but just how faithful it was to Alberti's original project is a moot question. Between 1597 and 1600 Antonio Maria Viani added the crypt, the sanctuary and the arms of the transept (the vaulting here dates to between 1697 and 1710), while it was not until between 1732 and 1782 that the dome, later decorated by Paolo Pozzo, was built to a design by the architect Filippo Juvarra.

Preceding page: *House of Giovanni Boniforte da Concorezzo, facade (15th cent.).*

Left: *facade of the Basilica of Sant'Andrea.*

Pages 74-75: *the Basilica of Sant'Andrea seen from Piazza Leon Battista Alberti.*

Three hundred years that lapsed between the original design and the final realization, make it impossible to know what Alberti's original model looked like. The solutions adopted in the apse and the transept are in any case highly questionable.

The first problem encountered in an attempt to interpret the building is the facade, in the form of a Roman triumphal arch (like that of Janus). Some maintain that the vestibule (pronaos) before the facade of the church itself was not part of Alberti's concept, as would also seem to be demonstrated by the unresolved great arch which rises up over the upper part of the facade (and the purpose of which is not clear). Inside this pronaos, covered by fine barrel vaulting based on antique examples (even if the stucco coffers were added in 1832), is the sixteenth-century entrance door to the basilica, also inspired by antique motifs.

The great monumental interior, airy and sumptuous with rich polychrome decoration, as it is now is on a Latin-cross plan, with a nave and square side chapels alternating with smaller chapels covered by cupolas. This idea of a single hall with side chapels is typical of Alberti and was later frequently adopted in sixteenth- and seventeenth-century architecture. The side chapels, like the nave, are covered by coffered barrel vaulting while light streams in from the great eighteenth-century dome. The decorations of the

Basilica of Sant'Andrea. Above: *view from the side with the bell tower.*

Right: *detail of the triumphal arch at the entrance.*

nave were begun by pupils of Mantegna, then continued in the sixteenth century by pupils of Giulio Romano, to be followed in Neoclassic times by Giorgio Anselmi (1723-1797) and various artists of the Accademia di Belle Arti in Mantua (directed by Felice Campi). The last touches were put on in the nineteenth century.

The first chapel on the right, used as a baptistery, is very sober in the lack of decoration, with three detached fresco tondos from the vestibule of the Basilica on the walls: the *Holy Family* and the *Deposition* by Antonio Allegri known as Correggio (1489-1534), and an *Ascension*, by followers of Mantegna. The walls in the second chapel have a series of frescoes depicting *Paradise, Purgatory and Hell*, by Benedetto Pagni (1525-1570), a follower of Giulio Romano, while in the third chapel is an altarpiece with *Madonna and Saints*, dating to the late fifteenth century, of Lombard school.

In the fourth chapel are frescoes by Andreasino, while the altar consists of a sixteenth-century decorative ensemble with sacred representations referring to the *Virgin*.

In the sixth chapel is an altarpiece with the *Nativity*, a sixteenth-century copy of a painting by Giulio Romano, while the frescoes, also on a design by Romano, with the *Crucifixion* and the *Discovery of the Most Precious Blood* are by Rinaldo Mantovano. The sarcophagi on either side of the altar contain the relics of Longinus, the saint who brought the blood of Christ to Mantua, and of Saint Gregorius Nazianzeno.

Basilica of Sant'Andrea. Left: detail of a candelabrum on the left side of the entrance arch.

Below: interior.

One of the four staircases, set into the piers which support the dome, takes us to the crypt, a Greek cross plan with three aisles in Tuscan order, built at the end of the sixteenth century by Antonio Maria Viani.

The small temple at the crypt crossing was built in 1818 and the relic of the Most Precious Blood is set on the altar in an ark decorated with a bas-relief in bronze. Seventeenth-century altars are in the arms of the crypt.

Back in the church, in the right arm of the transept, a chapel opens off on the right, containing a series of tomb monuments from various deconsecrated churches in the city. There are three niches in the back wall of the transept. The one in the center contains the mausoleum of Giorgio Andreasi of 1549, while on either side are large cupboards, part of the nineteenth-century furnishings of the basilica. The Chapel of the Holy Sacrament, decorated with two paintings by Felice Campi, is on the left wall of the transept, while the eighteenth-century altar has an altarpiece by Felice Niccolini.

The great dome designed by Juvarra rises over the crossing. It rests on a large drum which has twelve windows framed by Corinthian pilasters, and at its zenith is eighty meters high. The *Glory of Paradise* in the dome was painted by Anselmi between 1777 and 1782 in line with the sumptuous decorative taste of

Basilica of Sant'Andrea. Above: detail of one of the pilasters and the nineteenth-century vaulting inside. Below: *eighteenth-century dome by Juvarra.*

late Baroque inspiration. In the transept, below the dome, is a large Neoclassic octagonal prie-dieu, located so that the small temple below with the Holy Relic at the center of the crypt can be worshipped.

The high altar in the sanctuary was built in 1803 by Paolo Pozzo who set two finely sculptured Renaissance marbles at either side as demonstration of the fact that the basilica furnishings were continuously being moved from one place to another.

The choir stalls and the organ are set against the sanctuary walls, while a fresco with the *Martyrdom of Saint Andrew* by Anselmi is in the conch of the apse. The statue of *Duke Guglielmo Gonzaga*, praying, to the left of the altar, dates to 1572.

The right-hand chapel in the left arm of the transept contains a seventeenth-century altarpiece by the Bolognese painter Giovan Battista Caccioli, while a side exit at the end of the transept leads to Piazza Leon Battista Alberti, where the old Benedictine monastery once stood. This entrance too has a vestibule outside similar to the one on the main facade of the Basilica, but in this case unfinished and by some held to be earlier.

To be noted above, to the right and left, two large volutes, also unfinished, which bear witness to the intention to provide this part of the building with a structured facade, probably in the Baroque period.

Back in the left transept of the church, the chapel on the right also contains various tomb monuments. Of note in the center is the *Andreasi-Gonzaga Mausoleum*, thought by many to be by Giulio Romano and also modeled on an ancient triumphal arch. The *Strozzi Mausoleum* of 1529 is set against the right wall, supported by caryatids whose obvious antiquarian character also brings to mind Giulio Romano, while seventeenth-century frescoes decorate the walls.

The first chapel from the back, on the left side of the Basilica hall, has an altarpiece with the *Crucifixion*, painted in 1556 by Fermo Ghisoni, a pupil of Giulio Romano, while tombs are depicted on the walls.

Outside is a sculptured marble pulpit, dating to the early sixteenth century. Frescoes by Lorenzo Costa the Younger with scenes of the *Nativity* line the walls in the third chapel while the large wooden altarpiece and the two painted panels are attributed to Giovan Battista Viani (although the panels might be earlier, in which case they might be by Andreasino). In the fourth chapel, one of the small ones with a dome, there are medallions by the school of Mantegna in the pendentives and in the cupola, examples of the sixteenth-century decoration right after the new basilica had been built.

The painting with the *Madonna Enthroned*, dated 1525, in the fifth chapel is by Lorenzo Costa the Elder, while the sixth and last small chapel holds the tomb of Andrea Mantegna, buried beneath the floor in 1506. On the left, next to the entrance door is the lovely bronze *bust of Mantegna* with an intense expression, set on a porphyry disk framed in marble with arabesque designs, which may have been made by Mantegna himself. The paintings on the walls are by the school of Mantegna (the *Deposition, Baptism of Christ* and the *Holy Family with John the Baptist and other saints*), as are the frescoes on the walls, on the pendentives and in the small cupola, probably done on cartoons designed by Mantegna, and attributed in part to the young Correggio.

The panel with the *Holy Family* on the back wall is also connected with Mantegna's production. This chapel is one of the finest and most interesting spaces in the entire basilica.

Basilica of Sant'Andrea.
Above, left:
Pendentive in the dome; right:
bronze Bust *of Andrea*

Mantegna (15th-16th cent.).

Above: *view of the Basilica with Juvarra's dome.*

(Corso Umberto I)
Piazza Marconi

The triangular Piazza Marconi is located along one of the oldest thoroughfares of the historical city, to which the Renaissance porticoes still to be seen on two sides bear witness.

The house at n. 14 has an extremely interesting fifteenth-century painted facade, of which we know much more after recent restoration (1995). There is a frieze with putti at the top, while a series of panels with fine frescoes also decorated the lower part. Fragments of frescoes on the contiguous buildings indicate that this house, with arcading on the ground floor and fine fifteenth-century capitals, originally continued at the sides. The decoration with putti, ribbons and racemes below the cornice had previously already suggested the milieu of Andrea Mantegna and his pupils, in particular Correggio, whom we know to have been active in the church of Sant'Andrea nearby. Recent restoration however has revealed the existence of a scene on the facade below the frieze, showing a sovereign in a military camp, with tents, dignitaries and men in armor. The tense expressions and the spatial layout tie it in with Mantegna's activity in the early sixteenth century.

The inscription below, in Latin letters, celebrates the "*placabilitas*" and the "*clementia*", two qualities the first century A.D. writer Q. Curtius Rufus attributed to Alexander the Great. The figures in the scene could therefore be the Macedonians on the right with the Persians taken prisoner after the battle of Issus on the left. Below, in correspondence to the first floor, there were depictions of various buildings of a city, perhaps Alexandria of Egypt, certainly however identified with Mantua, with a triumphal arch like the one on the fountain of Sant'Andrea.

Other buildings depicted might be related, more generally, to projects by Leon Battista Alberti: in addition to Sant'Andrea, the Tempio Malatestiano in Rimini and other models. The house certainly was not an ordinary dwelling, but appears to be the one described in documents as ceded to Francesco Gonzaga by Andrea Mantegna, who had decorated it, and the "*clementia*" of Alexander the Great would therefore also be an attribute of the Marchese.

Facade of the house in Piazza Marconi 19. Below: detail of the frieze (15th-16th cent.).

LOGGIA DEI MERCANTI and PALAZZO DELLA CAMERA DI COMMERCIO (Merchants' Loggia and Chamber of Commerce Building)

(via Calvi)

The Chamber of Commerce building was begun in 1913 by the Mantuan architect Aldo Andreani (1887-1971) whose eclectic taste associated elements of Art Nouveau with references to neo-medieval historical styles, in line with late nineteenth-century concepts as to what a Loggia for Merchants should look like.

What Andreani was proposing here was "the market Palace with loggia typical of the fourteenth and fifteenth centuries", where the "neo-Romanesque" and above all "neo-Gothic" styles were fused into an astonishing cascade of shimmering polychrome decorative elements, with hints of Art Nouveau orientalizing taste.

What prevails in Andreani's work is the extreme attention paid to the "fragment", where the achievement of an elegant refinement depended on the care taken in handling details, the individual components, texture, all features which were then fused into a complex whole marked by the contemporary presence of diverse styles and artistic influences, the end result of a highly erudite mind encompassing a vast range of fields and knowledge.

Loggia dei Mercanti (1913).
Above: *the atrium.*
Left: *the facade.*

Former Jewish Ghetto

The Jewish ghetto was instituted in the early seventeenth century in this part of the city. The area was surrounded by high walls and had four archways, which were locked at night. The segregation imposed on a community which had been in the city for centuries, combined with its prosperity, led to considerable changes in the traditional types of dwellings. The high building density in fact determined the development of houses that expanded upwards and in which more than one family lived, and where the economic well being was revealed by portals and balconies with differing degrees of decoration. In the nineteenth century and above all after 1904 a series of reclamation projects led to the demolition of buildings and entire city blocks, which greatly modified the aspect the city had acquired after the formation of the ghetto, and only a few important examples survived to bear witness to that period.

PALAZZO DEL RABBINO
(Palace of the Rabbi)

The Rabbi's Palace is one of the most interesting examples of what the houses in the old ghetto looked like. Built at the end of the seventeenth century, perhaps to a design by the Flemish architect Frans Geffels (known from 1635 to 1699 and architect of the neighboring Palazzo Sordi), the house has a series of stucco panels on the facade, of rather modest craftsmanship, including a *Depiction of Mantua* or of perhaps biblical *Ideal Cities*. To be noted is the rich rusticated portal with diamond faceted ashlars like those at the corners of the palace and the window jambs.

(Via Pomponazzo)
PALAZZO SORDI

The long facade of Palazzo Sordi, built for the family of the Sordi marchesi by the Flemish architect Frans Geffels in 1680, is finely decorated. The rich and complex composition which distinguishes it is typically Baroque in its alternation of solid walls and empty spaces on the window axes. The two-tier facade is articulated by a series of coupled openings both horizontally (with pairs of close-set windows), and vertically (thanks to the insertion of a balustrade at the level of the string course). Below, pilaster strips - consisting of alternatively smooth and rusticated ashlars, surmounted by a coat of arms - articulate the composition with an increase in openings and decorative elements near the portal (over which is a tondo of the *Madonna and Child* by Giovan Battista Barberini). The bust of the patron, the Marchese Benedetto Sordi, is on the right corner of the building.

To be noted inside is the imposing staircase, one of the finest in Mantuan Baroque, richly decorated with putti and vases, also by Giovan Battista Barberini (1625-1691). The lovely courtyard is distinguished, on the facade of the central nucleus of the

Palazzo Sordi, facade (1680).

palace, by a rich decorative ensemble which has two large herms in correspondence to the large round-arched window in the center of the *piano nobile* or main floor. These figures support a rich frieze decorated with spirals and, above, statues in niches.

Of great interest on the piano nobile are the two "rooms of honor", decorated with stuccowork and frescoes, known respectively as dell'*Età* and of *Belgrade*.

PALAZZO DELLA FINANZA

The building, originally a convent, was completely renovated in 1787 by Paolo Pozzo with a facing in Neoclassic style within which the artist set two sixteenth-century portals.

One of these came from the demolished convent church, the other, attributed to Giovan Battista Bertani (1516-1576), from the former headquarters of the customs building.

Above, right: *Church of S. Martino, facade (1737).*

Palazzo della Finanza.
Left: *detail of the portal (attributed to G.B. Bertani).*
Below: *cloister of the old Carmelite convent.*

Two late fifteenth-century cloisters in two tiers still exist inside, while a late Gothic cornice from the convent church can be seen in the adjacent Vicolo del Carmine.

CHURCH OF SAN MARTINO

The original medieval building, which formed the nucleus of the Church of S. Martino, was completely rebuilt in 1737, with an extremely austere facade, animated by aedicules containing statues of saints at the sides, a relief of *St. Martin on Horseback and the Beggar* over the central portal, and the unique curved pediment above.

The interior, decorated in stuccowork, has a series of paintings over the altars of which two are of particular note. To the right of the choir is *St. Martin Dividing his Cloak*, by Ippolito Castagna (1506-1561), while an altarpiece with the *Madonna and Child with Saints*, from the workshop of Lorenzo Costa the Elder (1450/60-1535), is on the third altar to the right.

Right: *the Rio seen from Via Trieste.*

Facing page, left: *the Rio seen from Piazza Cavallotti;* right: *the Rio seen from Via Pescherie.*

The Rio

Between 1188 and 1190 the City of Mantua had the old Roman and early medieval city center enlarged beyond what is now Piazza Sordello. Reorganization of the waterways by the engineer Alberto Pitentino was part of this imposing project. The course of the Mincio river was broadened out to form what is now the Lago Superiore, and the so-called Rio was laid out at the same time. The Rio is an urban canal which connected the new body of water with the Lago Inferiore, on the east (also the result of widening the course of the Mincio). It was in other words a sort of moat which bordered the newly founded *civitas nova*, included within the second circle of city walls. Mantua, in addition to looking like a "water city" as was the case in many centers of the Po Valley, cut through by rivers and canals, now looked like an actual island in the bed of the river Mincio, bordered further south by still another large lake, the Lago di Paiolo, drained in the eighteenth century. The Rio, in addition to being an important urban boundary, was also a vital connecting axis for river traffic and therefore a real water trade route, along which pre-industrial productive activities arose, and which culminated westwards, overlooking the Lago Superiore, in a

Franciscan settlement, dated 1220. On the east the Rio flowed into the Porto Catena, used from the thirteenth century on as a river port. The first important interventions aimed at transforming the island-city Mantua took place in the early 1900s with the draining of Lake Paiolo, the filling in of the Fossa Magistrale (on the southwest) and, above all, the partial filling in of the middle stretch of the Rio, which was not concluded till the 1950s. Only a few partial, fascinating views of the old river canal still exist.

CASA DI GIOVAN BATTISTA BERTANI (House of Giovan Battista Bertani)

In 1554 the duke's architect, who had become fairly prosperous thanks to the prestigious commissions received from the court, bought an old building that stood on this parcel to change it into a house for himself. In two years the work was terminated and in a treatise published in 1558 Bertani described some of the details he had designed for this house of his, as examples of how the Ionic order should be built. Unfortunately the building has been modified throughout the centuries, including the facade, on which however there are still some unique marble reliefs regarding the construction of decorations in the Ionic order. Next to the entrance portal are two columns, complete with pedestals and entablature, which were originally finished like "bronze", as Bertani affirms. One is complete, in high relief, while the other is a cross section "engraved with all the measurements". Giorgio Vasari was struck by this didactic "decoration" and mentioned it as early as 1568. Two plaques are situated next to these reliefs, with the one under the right window prescribing the correct system for designing an Ionic door according to Vitruvius. The plaque under the left window shows the door itself, indicating the names of all the components. A fire broke out in 1738 and in the nineteenth century the various elements of the facade were recomposed, and a marble plinth was added, which unfortunately makes it difficult to see the prescriptions in Bertani's reliefs. The position of the plaques has also been reversed.

Even so it is a noteworthy and practically unique example of the residence of a Renaissance artist, who turned his theoretical studies into a manifesto of his program and aesthetic principles as well as a sort of *status symbol*.

(via Gori)
SINAGOGA NORSA (Norsa Synagogue)

The building that served as the ghetto synagogue in 1702 was subsequently destroyed. In 1904 it was completely rebuilt on the model of the old Synagogue (a few original pieces and above all a Holy Ark are inside).

(Via Massari - Via Filippo Corridoni)
CHURCH OF SANTA MARIA DELLA CARITA'

The church of Santa Maria della Carità, completely rebuilt in 1613 on the site of an old medieval building to which the bell tower alone bears witness, stands enclosed in a small church square which houses a collection of inscriptions and reliefs found in the territory of Mantua.

The eight unusually shaped eighteenth-century canvases on the walls inside, with *Scenes from the Old and New Testaments*, are by Giuseppe Bazzani.

Ovals in tempera by the same artist are in the vault, depicting the *Theological Virtues*, while to be

noted on the second altar on the left, a sixteenth-century altarpiece by Domenico Brusasorci with the *Martyrdom of San Biagio* and, over the third altar, a *Madonna and Child with Saints*, painted by Giovanni Canti in the eighteenth century. In the sanctuary is an early sixteenth-century painting of the *Archangel Michael and Saints* by the Veronese artist Giovan Francesco Caroto (1480-1555).

(Via Pescherie)
PESCHERIE (Fish market)

Work on the present building which crosses over the Rio, and which may originally have been a fish market, was begun in 1546, adjoining the new Beccherie, situated along the canal, and built in 1536 on a project by Giulio Romano, to replace the old meat market near the ghetto. The complex, which consisted of two structures at right angles to each other (the Beccherie was torn down in 1877 with the exception of the ground floor pylons along the Rio), immediately became known for its functionality and hygiene, for the waters of the canal ran along inside.

Still standing is the structure across the Rio, a sort of porticoed passageway with rusticated arcading and

Preceding page, left: *House of G. B. Bertani, facade (16th cent.).* Right: *Church of S. Maria della Carità, facade.*

Above: *the Pescherie.* Below: *the pylons of the new Beccherie on the Rio; in the background the Pescherie and the bell tower of the church of S. Domenico (demolished).*

an attic, articulated by rectangular windows. Some of the bracket reliefs in the attic are in the style of Giulio Romano.

ITINERARY 3

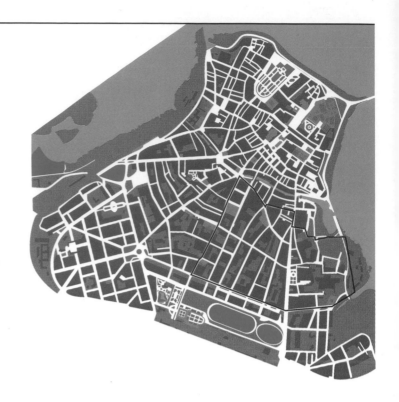

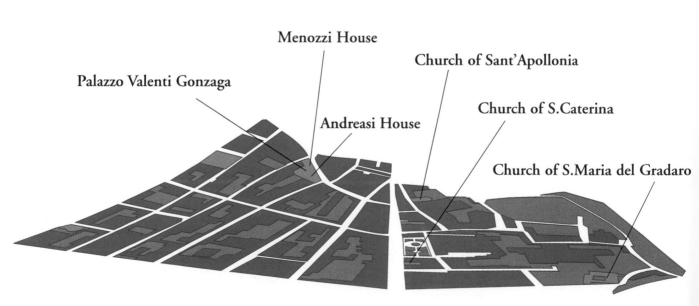

Palazzo Valenti Gonzaga

Menozzi House

Andreasi House

Church of Sant'Apollonia

Church of S.Caterina

Church of S.Maria del Gradaro

The south quarters: "Giulio's Addition"

Via Giulio Romano is the spine of a quarter built from scratch in the sixteenth century and known as "Giulio's Addition" for it was traditionally designed by Giulio Romano for this area inside the third circle of walls (finished in the fifteenth century) which had not yet been built up. It is in any case a planned expansion, with streets at right angles and with Via Mazzini functioning as a link between the medieval city and the new quarter, where tall residential buildings of notables sprang up. In the background were the Pescherie, also designed by Giulio Romano across the Rio.

In 1925 demolition in the area where Via Mazzini crosses Via Matteotti, left a great hole in the city fabric, previously occupied by the complex of the church of San Domenico, while the so-called medieval Trident (Via Benzoni, Via Trieste, Via Gandolfo) marked the northeastern limits of the "Addition" and the Lago Inferiore, and Via Frattini and Via XX Settembre marked the northern boundary.

(Via XX Settembre - Via Pietro Frattini)
CASA MENOZZI (Menozzi House)

The building dates to the second half of the fifteenth century and is probably on a design by Luca Fancelli, identifiable only in the upper floor of the

facade, where terra-cotta statues (the originals are now in the Ducal Palace) were set inside five aedicules, each framed by two engaged columns in brick, an unusual example of formal qualification of an otherwise ordinary facade.

PALAZZO VALENTI GONZAGA

Renovation of the Palazzo Valenti Gonzaga began in the early seventeenth century, when Nicolò Sebregondi, (1580/90-1652) designed the rich facade with five orders of windows above a fine ground floor base of diamond-faceted marble ashlars, creating a

Palazzo Valenti Gonzaga. Above: facade, seen from the inner courtyard. Left and above: details of the sculptural decoration.

Far left: Menozzi House, detail of the terra-cotta frieze with aedicules and statues (15th cent.).

fine contrast in color and light catching qualities with the wall of the upper part. The courtyard, in which the Flemish artist Frans Geffels also probably had a hand, has a rich stucco decoration by Giovan Battista Barberini (1625-1691), who ornamented the windows with spirals, cartouches, modillions, volutes. The same artist also decorated the rooms inside, also with a wealth of stuccowork as well as scenic frescoes.

CHURCH OF SANT'EGIDIO

The church of Sant'Egidio was rebuilt in the eighteenth century over a medieval building, as part of the general renovation of this portion of Mantua under Austrian rule.

The rich facade stands out in the city panorama, both in height and in the wealth of stucco reliefs and, above all, the rhythmical articulation of the central portion, surmounted by a large medallion under a curved pediment.

To be noted inside, on the second altar on the right, is a *Deposition with Cardinal Ercole Gonzaga* by Ippolito Costa (1506-1561), and a painting of the *Madonna and Child with Saints* by Benedetto Pagni (1525-1570), a pupil of Giulio Romano, in the

Cappella Magnaguti. Lastly, behind the high altar is a canvas with the *Martyrdom of Saint Vincent*, a fine painting by Giuseppe Bottani dating to 1776.

CASA ANDREASI (Andreasi House)

This house once belonged to a notable family of Mantua, the Andreasi. Attributed by some to Luca Fancelli, it is a fine example of domestic architecture of the second half of the fifteenth century The ground floor is of unplastered brickwork with a round-arched entrance portal. Above the facade are three rows of windows. The building is now a museum dedicated to the Blessed Osanna Andreasi (1449-1505), a Dominican lay sister whose life was entirely devoted to penitence and contemplation.

The Blessed Andreasi was highly esteemed by the Gonzaga family and was charged not only with seeing to the care of Margherita of Bavaria and her children when Federico I was away, but she replaced him in the government of the State as well. She also became a close friend of Isabella d'Este.

The Marchesi continuously asked for her advice and the Beata, according to her biographers, "listened, advised, directed".

She was subject to mystical ecstasies from childhood on and was known throughout Lombardy for her sanctity and ceaseless activity in favor of widows, orphans, the poor and friars and nuns. Pope Leo X, thanks to the intercession of Isabella d'Este, granted permission for her worship. Isabella also had a rich mausoleum built for her in the church of San Domenico, now torn down.

The Andreasi house is organized around a small inner court divided by a transverse portico on columns with the family coat of arms on the capitals. The upper rooms, which contain sixteenth-century frescoes, are now a museum and site of prayer.

(Via Gandolfo - Via Trieste - Via Fondamenta)
Porto Catena

The small and rather disorderly basin which now constitutes the Porto Catena gives us a very vague idea of what it was like when it was used as trading center as early as the fourteenth century, and closed by a chain (whence the name, catena = chain), exploiting an inlet of the Lago Inferiore into which the Rio had also been diverted.

The urban fabric of the surrounding streets, dating to the Middle Ages, was at the time occupied by merchants and warehouses, so that this area was extremely vital in the life of the city.

(Piazza Anconetta - Via Benzoni)
CHURCH OF SANT'APOLLONIA

The original medieval building was renovated between 1780 and 1799 by Paolo Pozzo, while the facade dates to 1834. The various interesting works inside include a *Madonna and Child*, of the first half of the sixteenth century, attributed by some to Lorenzo Costa the Elder, and an altarpiece with the *Holy Family and Saints*, by Giuseppe Bottani (1717-1784) from Cremona on the high altar, at the back of the apse.

(Corso Giuseppe Garibaldi)
CHURCH and MONASTERY OF SANTA PAOLA

The monastery of Santa Paola was built in 1416 on commission by the rulers of Mantua, in particular Paola Malatesta, wife of Gianfrancesco Gonzaga.

The convent church in late Gothic style (not open to worship) and a Renaissance cloister were part of the complex.

CHURCH OF SANTA CATERINA

The bell tower is all that is left of the original medieval structure. The church was completely renovated in 1738 and the peculiar theatrical facade dates to this time. The characteristic concave movement of the

facade makes it one of the most significant examples of Late Baroque in Mantua. The central portion, treated as if it were the tall baldachin of an altar, and the series of broken curvilinear pediments enrich the surfaces, and contribute to the animated effect of the whole.

Preceding page, left: *Church of Sant'Egidio, facade;* right: *Room of the Blessed Andreasi in the Andreasi House.*

Top: *Church of Santa Paola* (15th cent.).
Above: *Church of Santa Caterina, facade* (1738).

CHURCH OF SANTA MARIA DEL GRADARO

The monastery complex of Santa Maria del Gradaro was begun in the late thirteenth century (1256-1295) on the traditional site of the martyrdom of Longinus, the Roman soldier who after his conversion brought earth soaked with the blood of Christ from Calvary in Jerusalem (the holy relic of Sant'Andrea). Signs of the heavy-handed modifications to which the church was subject in the course of centuries (in 1772 the Austrian troops used it as a warehouse) are already apparent on the facade. Its present aspect is the result of the 1966 restoration and entire parts of the facade have been completely rebuilt (such as the overhanging roof and the two large pilasters), revealed by the brighter color of the bricks. The result is a mixed style within which Romanesque elements (justified by the date 1295 and the paternity of the portal by the Veronese architects "Magister Jacobus Gratasoia/Ognaben eius socius de Verona") can be found side by side with Gothic elements, such as the arches of the portal and the two very tall windows at the sides, while the large rose window dates to the early fifteenth century.

The interior has a nave and two side-aisles subdivided by columns in the front and by pilasters towards the apse. Originally a screen (iconostasis), of which traces are still visible, divided the space into a church for the faithful and a portion reserved for the friars. The side chapels, dating to the sixteenth century, are separated by coupled columns along the aisle walls.

In the apse (originally the monks' choir) there are interesting Byzantine frescoes, bordered by decorative bands, with *The Last Supper* and *Bishops, Apostles and Saints*, of the late thirteenth century, stylistically influenced by Venetian mosaic decoration of the same period. A room to the left of the sanctuary also contains the remains of slightly later frescoes, once more with figures of Saints.

Of particular interest in the monastery is the fifteenth-century cloister with arcading closed on one side by a structure built on an earlier complex in 1454 and later.

(Via Giu
PALAZ

The
loveliest

century
probabl
therefoi
periphe
city as
The
are still
particu
a proje
Palazzo
inal co
sources
have be
In 156
Roman
stables
buildin
exclude
the gre
ry aim
princeli
tures fr
ible hei
(accom
spent h
a new
work v
built. 1

(Piazza dei Mille - Via Giulio Romano - Via Vittorino da Feltre - Via Isabella d'Este)

CHURCH OF SANTO SPIRITO and CHURCH OF SAN LORENZINO

After a brief visit to the Church of Santo Spirito, in Via Vittorino da Feltre, which contains frescoes from the second half of the fifteenth century, the next stop is the church of San Lorenzino in Via Isabella d'Este.

The building, situated in an area behind the palace of the Petrozzani counts, was built in 1590 by Count Tullo Petrozzani, secret counselor of Duke Vincenzo I, both as a public oratory and private chapel.

The project for the building, generally attributed to Giuseppe Dattaro, known as Pizzafuoco (1540-1619), may possibly have been by the architect Antonio Maria Viani, in view of the close ties the Count had with the ducal family, and above all in view of the unusual elliptical plan with side niches based on a reproposal of Mannerist formal solutions. The simple facade of the church which is now served by the Comunità Evangelica Valdese, is characterised by four pilaster strips with Ionic capitals.

The slender pediment above has four small pedestals (acroteri) originally crowned by marble balls. The space inside is articulated by pilasters on high bases, which frame the four niches cut into the walls.

The statues of the *Evangelists* emerge from the predominating curved line which embraces the space and the movement of their garments add life to the surface.

Preceding page, top to bottom: *Cloister and Church of Santa Maria del Gradaro (14th-15th cent.).*

Left: *Church of San Lorenzino, facade (16th-17th cent.).*

(Via Giulio Romano - Via Giuseppe Mazzini)

HOUSE IN VIA MAZZINI N. 22

In its decorative reliefs, the facade of this house in Via Mazzini 22 is still another example of the popularity of the elegant antique motifs used by Leon Battista Alberti and his successors in the church of San Sebastiano.

These motifs were immediately adopted by builders in Mantua and used to ennoble the facades of domestic buildings.

What is of particular interest here is the terra cotta cornice dating to the fifteenth century and attributed to Luca Fancelli or, if earlier, to ideas furnished by Donatello (in which case this would not be an example of the "popularity" of Alberti's dictates, but an anticipation of them). The front and back part of the stone reliefs (plutei) in San Sebastiano, a complex to which this house is in any case closely related, are faithfully reproduced here.

CHURCH OF SANTA TERESA

The Church of Santa Teresa was built between 1668 and 1680 and is attached to the convent of the same name (used during Austrian rule as a place of consolation for those condemned to death).

The facade has an interesting portal with fine decoration, while to be noted inside is the sumptuous late Baroque decoration, which creates an all embracing space with luministic lighting.

On the first altar to the right is an altarpiece by Gerolamo Brusaferro of Verona dating to the eighteenth century, with *Saint John of the Cross*, a sixteenth-century mystic, while the large rich marble tabernacle set on the high altar constitutes a majestic scenographic apparatus.

The richness of the sanctuary is completed by the six paintings depicting *Scenes from the Life of Saint Theresa*, attributed to Filippo Gherardi and also dating to the late eighteenth century.

Right: *entrance with the sequence of doorways leading to the exedra.*
The doorways Giulio Romano designed for the Palazzo Te, with rusticated surrounds and architectural orders, were thought to be among the most successful examples of new monumental gateways for patrician palaces by Giulio's contemporary, Sebastiano Serlio.

Facing page, left: *Entrance atrium of the Courtyard: model of the complex of the Palazzo Te, as originally designed by Giulio Romano;* right: *Room of Ovid or of the Metamorphoses.*

The exterior, the original entrance and the present entrance

The three outer facades are all laid out on the same compositional scheme and make use of the same architectural idiom. Variations in detail however make some sides more important than the others.

The surface of these low masses - reinforced at the corners by a pier flanked by a "reinforcing" pilaster at the sides - is articulated by other pilasters of Tuscan order (the ideal architectural order for rustic buildings) which support an entablature of the Doric order. The spaces between one pilaster and the next are apparently clad in "rusticated" ashlars, or blocks of stone, more imposing below and more squared and less jutting above. Actually, architecturally speaking, this is a "pseudo-rustication" for what we have here is not real stone, but bricks clothed in a thin layer of plaster which simulates stone (in many cases however the eighteenth-century restorations have altered the sixteenth-century design of the rustication).

The most highly articulated facade is the one on the north, with three identical archways at the center, and four bays of windows on either side, only apparently symmetrical in arrangement, as was typical of Giulio Romano's projects. The entrance to the Palace, on the west side, through a large rusticated portal, leads into an atrium, derived from the one built shortly before 1525 by Antonio da Sangallo the Younger in the Palazzo Farnese in Rome. Giulio Romano, like Sangallo, wanted to repropose the vestibule which Vitruvius described as leading into the ancient Roman house, but like Sangallo, he too misunderstood the shape, building this space in aisles. From this entrance there is a fine view through the courtyard arches (which culminated in the seventeenth century with the construction of the exedra at

to have incorporated previous structures, as shown by some of the filled-in windows which do not correspond to the rooms inside (this also occurs on the outer facades). Giulio Romano's most important innovation concerns the architectural idiom, based on a sort of taste for the "precariousness" of all the decorative elements.

Although the combination of elements - niches, windows, pilasters and rustic stones - seems similar to that on the external facade of the Palazzo Te, here the pilasters have been transformed into engaged columns (elements which also articulated the courtyards of Villa Madama in Rome), and the triangular pediments over the windows are broken below, while in the Doric entablature above, the central decorative elements (triglyphs), done in 1533, seem to slide downwards as if the entablature itself were about to break.

This impression is also given by some of the keystones of the arched windows, which seem to fall inside the arch itself. These "precarious" architectural motifs were taken by Giulio Romano from Roman ruins of the ancient Basilica Aemilia, and here in Mantua were adapted to Mannerist architecture, to create a sort of game in the minds of the spectators, the feeling that the usual rules of static have been subverted. The entrance to the garden is on the left, with engaged columns and a triangular pediment, and a view of the great exedra at the back through the entrance arch.

the end of the garden), just as in the ancient Roman villas, on which Giulio Romano based this entire complex in Mantua.

Cortile d'Onore (Courtyard)

At the back is the great *Cortile d'Onore* or courtyard, one of the most interesting spaces in the whole palace, with four symmetrical facades overlooking its vast square plan. In various points these facades seem

Appartamenti delle Metamorfosi or of Isabella Boschetti

Back in the atrium, on the left, access on the right leads to a series of rooms which traditional assigns to Isabella Boschetti, the duke's mistress.

This is not confirmed by critics now, despite the fact that his long relation with the noble lady, niece of Baldassarre Castiglione, had even induced the duke to postpone his state wedding until 1531, arousing the wrath of the Marchesa Isabella d'Este.

Sala di Ovidio or delle Metamorfosi
(Room of Ovid or of the Metamorphosis)

The room takes its name from the wall frescoes painted by Agostino da Mozzanega and Anselmo de Ganis, on cartoons by Giulio Romano and inspired by Ovid's Metamorphoses.

Antiquarian references are not however limited to the stories narrated by the Latin poet, but also to the way in which they have been represented, obviously influenced by the Roman paintings discovered in those years in the Domus Aurea on the Palatine in Rome. The background of one of the frescoes, painted in 1527, shows a palace being built. It is probably

the Palazzo Te, thus furnishing us with valuable information as to how far the work had advanced at that date.

Stanza delle Imprese (Room of the Devices)

Known as the room of the "imprese", that is the Gonzaga devices supported by putti, which run along the frieze, the decoration was probably done to cartoons by Giulio Romano.

To be noted on the mantelpiece a bas-relief with the *Salamander* or *Green Lizard*, one of the devices frequently found in the main halls of the palace.

Left: *the fireplace in the Sala delle Imprese.*

Right: Sunset and the Moon.

Facing page, left: *Loggia delle Muse;* right: *detail of the south wall of the Sala dei Cavalli.*

Stanza del Sole e della Luna
(Room of the Sun and the Moon)

The ceiling is divided into rhombi containing stucco figures, probably by Primaticcio and Scultori. The fresco in the center depicts *Sunset*, in line with an iconographic scheme particularly suited to a living room. The cartoons were furnished by Giulio Romano, while the later stuccowork on the walls is part of the Neoclassic restoration.

La Loggia delle Muse

The name derives from the stucco muses in the vault, probably done by Francesco Primaticcio (1504-1570) and assistants, while the wall paintings are by pupils of Giulio Romano (Rinaldo Mantovano and Benedetto Pagni). The widespread use of stuccowork inside the Palazzo Te is probably due to the rediscovery in those years of many antique reliefs in stucco in the Domus Magna on the Palatine in Rome. They were then reproposed in detail in their antiquarian effect in Giulio Romano's works in Mantua. The lunettes contain paintings with *Hippocrene, the fount of the Muses*, and the *Nymph Castalia*, after whom this

room is named, while the Egyptian motifs on the vaulted ceiling may be before 1530. The decoration therefore identifies this part of the Palace as the wing for leisure and recreation, as the dwelling of the Muses and it corresponds to the Apartments of Isabella Boschetti, while in the *Loggia di Davide*, near the Ducal Apartments, the motifs are more martial. In the course of the latest restoration interesting architectural sketches were discovered on the outer wall of the Loggia. These include a corner of a villa with a loggia and, at the side, a Serlian window (a central arched window with flat-arch openings on either side), as well as sketches for subjects then painted in the *Sala di Psiche*.

State Rooms
Sala dei Cavalli *(Room of the Horses)*

After the Loggia delle Muse comes the Sala dei Cavalli, originally used as entrance hall for audiences and therefore one of the most solemn rooms in the palace, distinguished, unlike the other rooms, by the architectural orders on the wall, subdivided by frescoed Corinthian pilasters and with niches containing illusionistically painted statues. These pilasters frame large panels with six horses standing in front of landscape backgrounds. The Gonzaga were particularly fond of their horses which were housed in the stables that were here before the building of the Palazzo Te. Figures of pagan *Divinities* and scenes with the *Labors of Hercules*, all in a particularly sumptuous and monumental style, by Rinaldo Mantovano and Benedetto Pagni, on designs by Romano, and a frieze of putti and foliage complete the decoration. The fine painted coffered ceiling was done by Gasparo Amigoni in 1527-28 and the decorations in the coffers consist of rosettes alternating with the symbol of Mount Olympus, the dwelling of the Gods, alluding to the high peaks achieved by the Gonzaga, as shown by their superimposed crest.

Right: *Sala dei Cavalli.*

Facing page, top to bottom: *Room of Cupid and Psyche and detail of an erotic scene in this room.*

Pages 102-103: *Room of Cupid and Psyche,* The Wedding of Psyche and the Banquet of the Gods.

The pentagonal panels contain salamanders, accompanied by the motto "*ciò che a lui manca, tormenta me*" (what he lacks, torments me), alluding to the ardor to which the lizard was supposed to be immune and which inflamed the life of Federico for Isabella Boschetti.

Sala di Amore e Psiche (Room of Cupid and Psyche)

This room which was used for banquets has frescoes divided into compartments of various shape, with the *story of Psyche* as told in *The Golden Ass*, by the Latin writer Apuleius, which celebrates the power of Love. This is one of the most important and best known cycles in Italian Mannerist painting. The story begins in the ceiling, where in the right octagon Psyche is worshipped by men as a goddess for her beauty. Then comes the enraged Venus ordering Cupid to make Psyche fall in love with a horrendous man, followed by the prediction of the oracle of Apollo on the fate of Psyche, the girl abandoned on a cliff, Psyche asleep, the maiden at Cupid's table, the visit of her sisters and still other episodes. In the lunettes are the trials to which Psyche must be submitted for her arrogance, while the windowless walls have the *Wedding of Psyche and Cupid Celebrated on Olympus*, in which the fine elephant on the left and the dromedary led by an African on the right should be noted. The pictures on the other two walls refer to stories of gods and heroes, unrelated to the myth of Psyche, and perhaps derived from the *Hypnerotomachia Poliphili*. Detailed allegorical references are of course also present in all these scenes, perhaps dictated by Mario Equicola and Paolo Giovio, possibly illustrating Neoplatonic concepts regarding the ascent of the Soul from the difficulties of life (the labyrinth on the floor), through suffering and obstacles (the scenes on the walls and on the ceiling) up to the purification (the celestial realm at the center of the ceiling). Some however identify Psyche with Isabella Boschetti, Venus with Isabella d'Este, the Duke's mother, and Cupid as the Duke himself.

We know that the frescoes were completed in 1528 and the room could therefore not have been changed architecturally after that date since the panels fitted in between the windows and the brackets of the ceiling had already been set in place. The project must therefore have been very early, making it one of the first to be executed in the Palazzo Te. The iconography for this cycle was furnished by Giulio Romano while the magnificent composition itself was painted by Rinaldo Mantovano, Benedetto Pagni and Fattore, assisted, in the fine landscape backgrounds, by Luca da Faenza and Fermo da Caravaggio. The lower walls were once covered with tapestries and richly worked decorations, for painting was confined to the upper part of the walls. The room is an interesting mixture of architecture and decoration, both aimed at exalting Federico Gonzaga as the inscription in the frieze tells us (he had this room built "*in onesto ozio dopo le fatiche allo scopo di ristorare le energie per una vita di pace*" "in honest idleness after his efforts so as to restore the energies for a life of peace").

Preceding page: *Room of Cupid and Psyche.*
Above: *mythological scene (to be noted, on the left, one of Giulio Romano's typical Solomonic columns).*

Below: Venus and Mars at the Bath.

Above: *Room of the Zodiac.*

Left: Sign of the Ram *(detail).*

La sala dei Venti o dello Zodiaco
(Room of the Winds or of the Zodiac)

The ceiling is subdivided into panels and lozenges which contain frescoes or stuccoes of the *Gods*, the *Months* and the *Winds*. The sixteen medallions painted by Giulio Romano and assistants depict the *Horoscopes*, which represent the effects of the stars on human life as described by Firmicus Maternus, a Late Classic writer (whose work, *Matheseos*, Ludovico

*Room of the
Eagles or of
Phaethon,
details.*

Gonzaga had had copied from the collections in the *Biblioteca Malatestiana in Cesena* in 1461). The marble of the fireplaces and doorways adds to the magnificence of this Room, as in the Sala delle Aquile.

Private rooms
Sala delle Aquile or of Fetonte
(Room of the Eagles or of Phaethon)

This room has been identified as the bedchamber of Federico II and takes its name from the scene in the central octagon of the *Fall of Phaethon*. Amazons, Centaurs, Titans and Naiads are in the corners, while the shell niches contain Eagles. The stuccowork in the lunettes and friezes is particularly fine, while the central scene seems to have been painted by Giulio Romano in

Loggia Grande or of David, view by night.

Pages 108-109: *view of the east facade from the garden, with at the center the Loggia Grande or of David and the Peschiere.*

person. The name of Agostino da Mozzanega is mentioned for the mythological episodes, grotesques and battles, while Primaticcio did the stuccowork. To be noted over the mantelpiece, the usual two green lizards.

Loggia Grande or Loggia di Davide

In 1530 the Emperor Charles V, who raised Federico Gonzaga from Marchese to Duke, was received in this open space which connects the Cortile d'Onore with the garden. The paintings that decorate the room depict the *Stories of David*, king of ancient Israel, with his heroic deeds, his love for Bathsheba. This cycle, which is located next to the Duke's chambers, celebrates in allegorical key the martial virtues of Francesco Gonzaga, in

Sala degli Stucchi *(Room of the Stuccoes)*

Back in the Loggia of David, on the left is the entrance to the Sala degli Stucchi where the coffered barrel vault is decorated, like the lunettes, with stucco sculptures of mythological subjects.

The two-tiered frieze which decorates the top part of all the walls, usually attributed to Primaticcio and dated 1531, is remarkable. Some believe that the structure is a clear reference to the superimposed tiers of bas-reliefs in Trajan's Column in Rome, in line with a taste for the antique which Giulio Romano kept alive in Mantua after the presence of Alberti and Mantegna.

Below: *Room of the Stuccoes, details of the frieze.*

Right: *Room of the Caesars.*

Above: *detail;*

below: Caesar has Pompey's Letters Burned.

Sala dei Cesari or dell'Imperatore
(Room of the Emperors)

The name comes from the fresco in the center of the vaulted ceiling showing *Caesar having Pompey's Letters Burned*, while images of *Roman Emperors* and historical episodes, are to be found on the walls under a frieze of putti and divinities. They were considerably restored at the turn of the eighteenth century.

Sala dei Giganti *(Room of the Giants)*

This is certainly one of the best-known rooms in the Palazzo Te, mostly painted by Rinaldo Mantovano (but some say also by Giulio Romano) between 1532 and 1534, and also praised by Vasari. The decoration with the *Fall and Ruin of the Giants Struck by the Wrath of Zeus*, is a continuous scene from the vault to the walls creating an all embracing environment where even the floor, in river stones, was joined to the lower part of the walls, in line with a rich exuberant imagination which considered pictorial decoration and architectural effects one and the same thing. The subject, aimed at exalting the greatness of Charles V (*Jupiter*) with respect to his more titanic enemies (the *League of Cognac*), unfolds in a precipitant conflict of boulders, tumbling architecture and somber cataclysmic skies, in a sort of grandiose *capriccio*, the farthest possible from the studied balance and resoluteness of the Roman Classicist culture of Bramante and of Raphael, who had been Giulio's master. The flickering flames in the large fireplace once there reflected on the surfaces of the walls, accentuating the red-brown tones.

The acoustics here are also quite unusual and the sound waves bouncing off the ceiling amplify the voice from one corner to the one diagonally opposite.

*Room of the
Giants, details
of the vault.*

*Pages 114-115:
vault of the Room
of the Giants.*

113

Museo Civico

The Museo Civico has been installed on the upper floor of the Palazzo Te. The three interesting collections include the Egyptian collection, assembled by the Egyptologist Giuseppe Acerbi from Mantua in 1840 (to be noted in particular the *heads of Psamtik II, Ptolemy* and *Arsinöe*), the **Gonzaga Section** of numismatics with examples by Pisanello and the collection of weights and measures of Renaissance period with

Room of the Giants, Fall and Ruin of the Giants Struck by the Wrath of Zeus, *details.*

Ala napoleonica (Napoleonic wing)

After the Room of the Giants come a series of rooms redecorated in the early nineteenth century with stuccowork and grotesques.

fine decorations, and the **Galleria di Arte Moderna** with works in particular by Federico Zandomeneghi (1841-1917) and Armando Spadini (1883-1925).

Room of the Giants, mythological scenes in the vault.

- Church of San Sebastiano
- Mantegna's House
- Palazzo di San Sebastiano
- Palazzo di Giustizia
- House of Giulio Romano
- Church of San Barnaba
- Palazzo Aldegatti
- Church of San Maurizio
- Piazza Martiri di Belfiore
- Teatro Sociale
- Fifteenth-century corner pier
- Church of Sant'Orsola
- Church of Ognissanti
- Former San Clemente Clinic
- Church of San Francesco
- Private House
  (Via Fratelli Bandiera, 17)
- Palazzo Ippoliti di Gazoldo
- Palazzo Arrivabene
- Palazzo Canossa and Church of the
  Madonna del Terremoto
- Palazzo Barbetta
- Palazzo Guerrieri
- Palazzo Arrigoni
- Palazzo d'Arco
- Church of Santi Gervasio and
  Protasio
- Palazzo Cavriani and Garden
- Church of San Leonardo
- Piazza Virgiliana
- Museo Francesco Gonzaga
  or Museo Diocesano
- Palazzo del Seminario

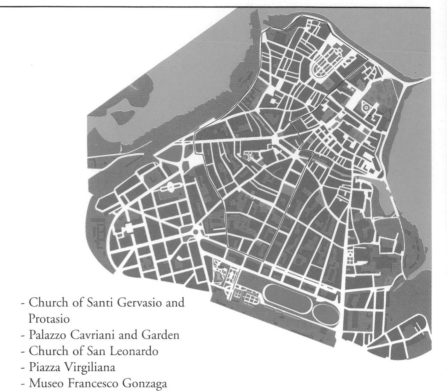

Palazzo d'Arco

Piazza Virgiliana

Church of San Francesco

Church of Sant'Orsola

Museo F. Gonzaga
or Diocesiano

Church of San Maurizio

Teatro Sociale

House of Giulio Romano

Palazzo di Giustizia

Mantegna's House

Church of San Sebastiano

(Via Giovanni Acerbi - Largo XXIV Maggio)
CHURCH OF SAN SEBASTIANO

The church of San Sebastiano, designed by Leon Battista Alberti in 1460, is another of the most important Renaissance churches, one of the first examples of the reproposal of ancient Roman architecture, in a humanistic key, where formal suggestions of various derivation however come together. The building has changed considerably as a result of the heavy restoration of 1925 which transformed it into a shrine for the war dead. The two large straight entrance staircases are part of this late restoration, and close off the two openings at the end of the crypt. The two entrance portals above were originally two windows with a fresco by Mantegna at the center of the facade where the plaque to the war dead is now located. Even so, traces of the pictorial decoration which covered most of the frieze and exterior of the church are still extant, although sadly deteriorated. The building was begun by Luca Fancelli in 1460, although it was not terminated until forty years later and we have no way of knowing how close it was to Alberti's model (in 1479, after the death of Ludovico, information on the construction yard seems to have ceased). The main floor of the church was raised and reached via two flights of stairs inside the small loggia on the left, while the old convent structure stood on the right. Changes made during the centuries however have succeeded only in part in jeopardising the striking innovations of this late phase of Alberti's vocabulary of forms, as demonstrated by his preference for solid walls rather than architectural orders. Actually we don't really know what the church looked like originally, except for the fact that Francesco Gonzaga, Ludovico's son, who commissioned the work, noted in 1473 that the building had certainly been conceived with "*garbo antico*", (in antique mode) but it was impossible to decide, in its strangeness, whether it was a "church or mosque or synagogue".

On the facade then we have a division into two levels with low openings below, a tall middle story, opened below by rectangular and semicircular openings, a large triangular frontispiece at the top. It has been suggested that the level of the lower arches had to do with a modification of the original idea where a large flight of steps, set frontally, led to the actual cella (as in Greek temples or the Roman podium temple). It has also been suggested that there may have been pilasters in the central plastered area of the facade, and not only at the corners and in the center. Whatever the case, particular note should be taken of the unusual composition of the frontispiece (despite the uniformity conferred by the coat of paint added

Church of San Sebastiano, as it was prior to its transformation in 1925.

in the 1900s). The horizontal movement is interrupted at the center by a window and an arch is inserted which moves up into the tympanum, an antique stylistic motif known as Syrian frieze. This motif was fairly common in antique monuments, and can be seen on imperial coins, or on the facade of Diocletian's palace in Split.

Not to be overlooked are the lovely fifteenth-century friezes with putti holding a garland which contains the sun (neoplatonic), set in the openings of the cella floor (there were two other stairs which corresponded to those there now), also outstanding examples of Alberti's love of the antique.

Inside too the reproposal of classic models is striking, with a Greek-cross plan taken from ancient burial monuments along the Via Appia in Rome and still extant in the fifteenth century. This ground plan was enormously popular in the late fifteenth and above all sixteenth century thanks to the example and thoughts of Alberti.

119

MANTEGNA'S HOUSE

This building, begun in 1476 according to the date cut into a marble cornerstone, is said to have been designed by Mantegna (who settled in Mantua in 1459), perhaps with the advice of Leon Battista Alberti. Construction actually continued for twenty years up to 1496, although radical restoration carried out in the course of the twentieth century has shown us what the house originally looked like. The large round courtyard, set within the square building, in particular reveals Albertian influences. A few late fifteenth-century designs by Francesco di Giorgio Martini also bear witness to this type, probably the result of an acquaintance with Alberti's ideas that came from his contacts with the intellectuals of the court of Lorenzo the Magnificent in Florence. Various rooms open off the court, in some of which traces of pictorial decoration are still visible, including the coat of arms of Ludovico II. The antique style reflected in Mantegna's house may have been carried even further by having this unusual cylindrical courtyard covered by a dome with an oculus for light at the center, almost a private miniature Pantheon.

Preceding page: Church of San Sebastiano. Above: facade; below: detail of a frieze in the transenna, with the Gonzaga coat of arms.

Mantegna's House. Above: exterior. Below, left: detail of the courtyard.

PALAZZO DI SAN SEBASTIANO

The former Palazzo di San Sebastiano stands between Largo XXIV Maggio and Viale Risorgimento. In 1506 Francesco II Gonzaga began restructuring and enlarging a pre-existent building adjacent to Andrea Mantegna's first house in the city (which the artist then left for the one described above). The Marchese decided to turn this complex near his stables on the Isola del Te (where the Palazzo would later be) into his new residence. San Sebastiano was then richly decorated by Lorenzo Leonbruno and Lorenzo Costa, who had come to the Court in Mantua in 1506, while the *Triumphs of Caesar* by Andrea Mantegna (now in Hampton Court) were located in the marchese's bedchamber.

The Palazzo had already been abandoned by 1536 and was frequently ill-used in the course of centuries. Some of the rooms still have part of their original decorations of a heraldic nature such as the devices of the crucible, of the candelabrum, or that of the sun, while most of the finest ceilings had already been dismantled by the late sixteenth century and are now in the Ducal Palace.

(Via Roma)
PALAZZO DI GIUSTIZIA

The building, probably on a design by Antonio Maria Viano, was built in the first two decades of the seventeenth century for a side branch of the Gonzaga family (the Gonzagas of Vescovado, in the Cremonese).

The facade is one of the clearest examples of Viani's love for variation in architectural decoration and in the use of chiaroscuro, probably because here the architect was working on a domestic building and not a public structure commissioned by the Gonzaga.

The vigorous basement, distinguished by flat strongly accentuated pieces of stone, contrasts sharply with the sculptural vigor of the twelve figures which rise from the pilasters like deformed Atlas figures supporting the Ionic capitals. The straight lintels over the openings below and the generous projecting entablature above accentuate the luministic effect of the entire composition. To be noted inside are the porticoed court and the main staircase decorated with fine stuccoes attributed to the workshop of Viani. Some rooms, such as the audience hall, had previously been decorated by pupils of Giulio Romano with frescoes of the *Seven Sages of Antiquity*, in illusionistic niches.

HOUSE OF GIULIO ROMANO

In 1524, when Giulio Romano arrived in Mantua in the entourage of Baldassarre Castiglione, the building that was to become his house already existed. His project dates to 1540, although the complex was subsequently enlarged and considerably modified, above all in the 1800s by Paolo Pozzo who changed the original proportions. Giulio completely remodelled the building, and the facade he designed is described by Vasari as "fantastic, all worked with colored stuccoes". Originally there were two windows on either side of the door. Giulio's idiom can still be seen in the rustic facing, the pedimented aedicules above the windows and the broken string course, all elements typical of the architect's works. A niche with a statue of *Mercury*, an antique restored in the sixteenth century, stands over the entrance portal. Inside is a spacious room with frescoes by Giulio Romano and his school, depicting *Classic Gods*.

(Via Chiassi)
CHURCH OF SAN BARNABA

The church of San Barnaba, dating to the Middle Ages, was completely rebuilt between 1716 and 1736 on a project by Doricilio Moscatelli Battagli (1660-

rich side altars and stuccowork were made by Stanislao Somazzi in 1768. Of note inside, to the left of the entrance, is a holy water font with Gonzaga devices in Carrara marble from the church of San Sebastiano; then come fourteen *Stations of the Cross*, an early work by Giuseppe Bazzani (1690-1769). A quatrefoil dating to 1760 and a picture by Lorenzo Costa the Younger (1537-1583) with the *Multiplication of Loaves and Fish* are on the inner wall of the facade. In the small Baptistery Chapel is a bas-relief with the *Resurrection of Christ* dating to the second half of the fifteenth century, while over the second altar on the left is a detached fresco, also late fifteenth century, with the Blessed Elisabetta Picenardi. At the back of the apse are a series of canvases by the school of Giulio Romano.

Next to the church are the remains of the fourteenth-century cloister, brought up to date in the fifteenth century with Renaissance cornices and supporting arches attributed to the milieu of Luca Fancelli.

Preceding page, left: *Palazzo di Giustizia;* right: *Giulio Romano's House*

Above: *statue of* Mercury, *set in the entrance portal of the House of Giulio Romano.*

Below: *Church of San Barnaba, facade (1716-1736).*

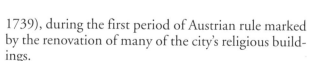

1739), during the first period of Austrian rule marked by the renovation of many of the city's religious buildings.

The facade, in a more monumental style, by Antonio Galli Bibiena, dates to 1737. The curved pediment of the large window touches the entablature above in a typically late Baroque variation of classical canons. The slender elongated obelisks at the sides, topped by pine cones, frame the central portion with a depressed arch frontispiece. The church has no side-aisles and a large dome is set over the sanctuary. The

PALAZZO ALDEGATTI

Via Chiassi is without doubt one of the most interesting streets in Mantua for it offers a sort of

compendium of the changing fashions and demands throughout the centuries as mirrored in the city's monuments and domestic architecture. A variety of stylistic approaches to the concept of facade exist within close reach of each other. One example is the house at no. 71 in Art Nouveau style, built in 1912 by Aldo Andreani, the outstanding representative of the new style in Mantua. Another is the Palazzo Cantoni Marca at no. 42, with a crowning that has been compared to Fancellian prototypes of the late fifteenth century but where the filled-in crenellations would seem to indicate a nineteenth- century neo-medieval interpretation, and the Baroque Palazzo Neri Bollati (now Scuola Media, at no. 62). The facade of Palazzo Aldegatti at no. 18, built in the first half of the sixteenth century, is distinguished by a fine marble portal. Inside, in the *main salone*, is a large frescoed frieze attributed to Andreasino (1548-1608) while the other rooms contain nineteenth-century decoration and bear witness to the decorative style of patrician houses in nineteenth-century Mantua.

CHURCH OF SAN MAURIZIO

Begun on a project by Antonio Maria Viani in 1609 and consecrated in 1616, the church did not receive its facade until 1731. The elliptical dome over the aisleless nave is unusual in the milieu of Mantua. Various interesting paintings are located in the Chapels. In the first chapel to the right is a detached fresco of the *Madonna Enthroned and Saints*, of the latter part of the sixteenth century as well as a painting of the same subject attributed to a follower of Ludovico Carracci; in the second Chapel is an *Annunciation* of 1616 by Carracci (1555-1619), who perhaps also painted the *Martyrdom of Saint Margarita* and *Beheading of the Saint* (works finished by Lucio Massari) in the third Chapel.

The sanctuary contains a series of canvases by the Flemish painter Jacob Denys, dating to the second half of the seventeenth century, depicting *Stories from the Life of St. Maurice*. In the second Chapel on the left to be noted are two paintings by Lorenzo Garbieri, also a pupil of Carracci, with the *Stories of Saint Felicita*, while in the first Chapel are works by the Mantuan Giuseppe Bazzani dating to the eighteenth century. Lastly to be noted on the right walls, the tomb inscription dictated by Paolo Giovio for Giovanni dalle Bande Nere who died in Mantua in 1526. It was originally in the church of San Domenico which no longer exists. At present the church is not open for worship.

Piazza Martiri di Belfiore

This is one of the most important and complete examples of town planning under the Fascist regime in Mantua aimed at renewing and adapting the architectonic facades of the city in line with the new style. In addition to the Palazzo del Consorzio Agrario Provinciale, note should be taken of the fine I.N.P.S. building with its angular form and treatment of the surfaces in travertine and masonry and with ornamental terra-cotta reliefs at the sides. This is a particularly important complex, related to a series of changes of a "modern" and rationalist type which involved replacing old buildings with new (the various former Fascist Party Houses (Case del Fascio) such as the one now used as barracks, the Caserma Luigi Boccaletti (Barracks) in Corso Garibaldi, or the one in Piazza Virgiliana, the schools in Via Solferino, the Dopolavoro building near the railroad station in Largo di Porta Pratella, and the buildings on the Corso della Libertà between Piazza Martiri di Belfiore and Piazza Cavallotti).

Preceding page, above: *House built on a design by Aldo Andreani, (1912);* below: *Church of S. Maurizio, facade (1731).*

Above: *two paintings of the* Martyrdom of Saint Margaret *(attributed to Ludovico Carracci, 1616).* Below: *INPS building.*

(Via Roma - Piazza Marconi - Corso Umberto I - Piazza Cavallotti)
TEATRO SOCIALE

The Teatro Sociale, one of the most significant Neoclassic theaters in Italy, was built between 1818 and 1822 on a project by Luigi Canonica (1762-1844), in a style frequently used in theater constructions. It was originally thought of as an opera theater, and was one of the most important works of public interest erected during the Austrian Restoration, for

the cultural qualification of the city of Mantua. The large portico (pronaos) is in the shape of a temple facade supported by six Ionic columns (hexastyle facade), with a spacious triangular frontispiece with garlands in the tympanum. The interior has five tiers of boxes and two in the gallery.

Behind the nineteenth-century railing, to the right of the Theater, is a small open space from which one can enjoy the most complete view of the Rio, the medieval canal opened by Alberto Pitentino.

(Corso Vittorio Emanuele II)
FIFTEENTH-CENTURY CORNER PIER
(Corner via Corrado)

Only a few decades had passed since Mantua became part of the Kingdom of Italy when, at the end of the nineteenth century, the government of King Umberto decided to completely renew Corso Vittorio Emanuele, which had become a key axis in the city, replacing the Renaissance buildings by new ones. In 1872 the church of San Giacomo was torn down and the fourteenth-century church of

Teatro Sociale (1818-1822), *facade and interior.*

Sant'Antonio was also demolished to make way for the Macello Comunale (City Slaughterhouse).

In 1905 the city walls began to come down, as well as the old city gates. A portion of the old Rio (created around 1100) was also covered over, while banks and new bureaucratic buildings sprang up along the new thoroughfare. This fifteenth-century corner pier with fine decoration was saved on account of its exceptional formal quality, to bear witness to the Renaissance decorative ensembles that characterized the houses of notables and which served as landmarks in the city.

CHURCH OF SANT'ORSOLA

In 1947, Via Bonomi, a new thoroughfare leading to the area of Lago Superiore, cut through the space once occupied by the old monastery of Sant'Orsola, torn down in 1930.

The only surviving part of the original complex is the convent church, built in 1608 by Antonio Maria Viani (1555/60-1629).

The octagonal ground plan, revealed externally by the tall windowed structure, is enclosed in a lower rectangular structure, with two facades. The main facade on Corso Vittorio Emanuele is articulated with coupled engaged columns set on high pedestals with aedicules in between and a spacious portal with a curved pediment. The side facade next to one side of the old monastery cloister is not nearly as complex and is articulated by simple bands. Inside the church, over the high altar, is a seventeenth-century painting.

In 1643 the duchess Maria Gonzaga had twelve prayer grottoes, as well as a cenoby for spiritual retreats, built. This hermitage, unfortunately deteriorated, is now in the gardens of the Circolo Ufficiali di Presidio (Officers Club), in Via Vittorio Emanuele. The two-story building has two flights of stairs on the facade.

Ten of the original twelve grottoes where the nuns retreated still exist, a unique urban example of Counter Reformation devotion which had led to the construction in isolated mountain sites in Northern Italy and Tuscany of "Sacri Monti", where the visit to various pavilions or grottoes constituted an itinerary of prayer and penitence. The purpose of this retreat was essentially the same, even though the site was urban.

Above: *detail of the corner pier in Corso Vittorio Emanuele (15th cent.).*

Left: *Church of Sant'Orsola (1608).*

CHURCH OF OGNISSANTI

The church of Ognissanti, to whose medieval origins the campanile and the chapel known as "dei Morti" (of the Dead) bear witness, was particularly important because of the adjoining hospital. In 1752-53 the facade of the building was redesigned in an austere late Baroque style which eschewed all ornamentation (with the exception of the aedicule pediment over the portal) but which still succeeded in bestowing a slightly concave movement to the facade, marked above by the curvilinear termination of the frontispiece.

Works of art inside the building include, on the first altar to the left, a sixteenth-century canvas with the *Preaching of St. John the Baptist* by the school of Giulio Romano, while there is a detached fresco with the *Madonna and Saints*, by Niccolò da Verona (active from 1462 to 1493), on the second altar on the right.

Of note in the sanctuary zone are a *Saint Benedict and Saint Clare* by Ippolito Andreasi (1548-1608) in the apse and a *St. John the Baptist*, attributed to the Roman painter Domenico Fetti (1589-1623).

On the left, in the Cappella dei Morti, the old abbots' mausoleum, are various fourteenth-century frescoes.

(via Nuvolari - Piazza Leoni - Via Solferino)
FORMER SAN CLEMENTE CLINIC

The building of the former San Clemente Clinic is located at no. 21 Via Solferino. The facade has a rich late Baroque decoration, in particular around the windows, with naturalistic elements, modillions, cartouches and cornucopias in relief which recall the style of Frans Geffels.

Church of Ognissanti. Above: facade.

Niccolò da Verona (1462-1493).

Clinic, facade (18th cent.); below: Church of S. Francesco.

Above, right: Madonna and Saints, fresco by

Facing page, above: former San Clemente

(Piazza San Francesco)
CHURCH OF SAN FRANCESCO

The church of San Francesco was built between the late thirteenth and early fourteenth century on the site of an oratory dedicated to one of the followers of Saint Francis, Friar Benvenuto. Its placement here, like that of the Dominican convent of San Domenico, exemplified the general concepts followed by the mendicant and preaching orders when they established their centers in medieval cities, choosing sites in the city outskirts that were rather densely populated but not yet an integral part of the urban fabric and where expansion was possible. In the case of the

Franciscan settlement in Mantua, this zone soon became a key point in the economic life of the city, since it was located right next to the Rio, an important waterway with installations relating to various productive activities (mills, fulling-mills, etc.) and, therefore, with the Lago Superiore. In the fifteenth century, the building, which had never been consecrated, became a key center of Gonzaga devotion, as was the case in a sense for all the Franciscan convents in the principal humanist courts of Central and Northern Italy, passing in 1436 from the Conventuals to the Observants, an affiliation of the Franciscan Order, under the protection of the Gonzaga (as was the case in Urbino, Florence, Ferrara). The church thus became no less than a mausoleum for the Gonzaga family, and in 1459 Pope Pius II, in Mantua for the famous Council called to declare a new Crusade, finally consecrated the building (Leon Battista Alberti was also in the city, in the Pope's entourage). The church was seriously damaged in the allied bombings in World War II, and was completely rebuilt. The apse has been reinvented and the facade is also an "invented" Lombard-Gothic style (post-war restoration based on old photos), with a fine marble portal at the center. In plan it is a basilica with a nave and two side-aisles separated by pointed, neo-Gothic arches. The austerity and the use of brick-work (not philological but which became fashionable

in the 1800s and is still in vogue) lend a "medieval" air to the interior. A series of chapels open into the right side aisle; in particular to be noted is the first on the right, spacious and deep, dating to the fifteenth century, which contains fragments of fourteenth-century funeral monuments found in the church. Above the side door are fragments of a fresco with *St. Francis*, by Stefano da Verona (1374-1438) and Domenico Morone (1442-1517) which furnish us with an idea, together with other remains here and there in the basilica, of what the interior of the church must have looked like in the Middle Ages and Renaissance with its fine decorative apparel (opposite are the detached synopia of the same fresco). In the second chapel is a wooden altar of the late sixteenth century, like the one in the fourth chapel, which however dates to the seventeenth century. In the fifth chapel, on the left, is a painting with St. Francis, attributed to Morazzone (1573-1626), in addition to a *praying Saint Francis*, of Venetian school, on the right. At the back, still on the right side, is the Gonzaga Chapel, where numerous members of the family were buried in the fourteenth and fifteenth centuries. Portions of frescoes dating to the 1360s and 1370s remain, while on the back wall is a depiction of *Saint Louis of Toulouse*, attributed to Tommaso da Modena (1326-1379) in which Luigi Gonzaga, first lord of the city, also appears. Of note in the left side-aisle, in addition to various remains of frescoes, is a late thirteenth-century depiction of the *Triumph of Death*.

Continuing up to where the Rio runs into the Lago Superiore, a fine view of this portion of the city can be had (to be noted, overlooking the canal, the Art Nouveau house built in the early twentieth century by Aldo Andreani).

(Via F.lli Bandiera)
PRIVATE HOUSE (via Fratelli Bandiera, 17)

The adoption of a whole series of ornamental ensembles in the principal buildings in Mantua by Leon Battista Alberti and his followers based on humanist concepts regarding relationships between geometric figures or the use of antique reliefs was soon reflected in domestic architecture.

The same thing can be said for the decoration of the school of Mantegna, which appears, albeit as excerpts, on the facade of the house in Via Fratelli Bandiera.

The large fascia below the eaves with putti on a gold ground over a sumptuous network of circles clearly reveals its origins in antique art, as a painted version of marble intarsia.

PALAZZO IPPOLITI DI GAZOLDO

In the first half of the eighteenth century the Palazzo Ippoliti di Gazoldo was built on the site of several medieval buildings. The facade is marked by its sloping buttress-like ground floor with small towers at the sides. Of great interest is the monumental staircase with stuccowork and rich marble decoration by Paolo Soratini (1682-1762).

PALAZZO ARRIVABENE

The palace, which belonged to the Arrivabene counts, was probably built to a design by Luca Fancelli, a pupil of Leon Battista Alberti, in the second half of the fifteenth century. To be noted in particular is the date 1481 cut into the elegantly sculptured corner pier, now on the large tower. Heavily transformed in the course of the centuries, Fancelli's design is revealed in the articulation of the various parts of the building around the square courtyard, with porticoes and a fine loggia above. The main staircase, as well as the entrance portal, date to the eighteenth century.

(Via Verdi)
PALAZZO COLLOREDO

This building is of some interest because in the nineteenth century it was attributed to Giovan Battista Bertani and by him *"egregiamente condotto su disegno di Giulio"* (excellently carried out on a design by Giulio) Romano.

(Piazza Matilde di Canossa)
PALAZZO CANOSSA and CHURCH OF THE MADONNA DEL TERREMOTO

The palace, commissioned by the aristocratic Veronese family Canossa, was built in the second half of the seventeenth century on the remains of another building. Aside from the nobility of its architectural parts, this patrician residence provides a clear example of how the syntax of Giulio Romano, introduced into Mantua more than a century earlier, continued to serve as model and was revisited by architects of the late seventeenth century. The horizontal development of the facade recalls that of the Palazzo Te, accentuated by the use of sham rustication and the triangular pediments over the windows, broken below for coats of arms, as in Giulio's idiom. This composition however does not repropose the innovations found in the Palazzo Te, for there are no pilaster strips. The portal at the center of the facade is clearly marked by the marble columns and the balcony, while there are two dogs, a Canossa symbol, at the base of the columns. To be noted the fine *Staircase*, one of the most mon-

Preceding page: *Corner tower of Palazzo Arrivabene.*

Above: *Church of the Madonna del Terremoto.*

Below: *Piazza Canossa and, on the left, Palazzo Canossa.*

Palazzo d'Arco, Sala delle Figurazioni Sacre. Right: Christ on the Cross, *by the workshop of Van Dyck.* Below, left: *view of the Sala;* right: *Room of the Still Lifes,* Christ with the Cross *(attributed to Sodoma).*

comprising the *Sala di Diana* (with seventeenth-century canvases such as *Juno, Ceres* and *Psyche* by Sante Peranda), the *Red Room*, with furniture of the second half of the nineteenth century, the *Sala di Pallade*, with a vaulted ceiling frescoed in the eighteenth century by Giovan Battista Marconi and Gaetano Crevola (to be noted the portrait of *Count Annibale Chieppo*, by some attributed to Rubens). These are followed by the *Sala della Giustizia* or *Sala Verde*, with a *Virgin and Child and Angels* on gold ground dating to the second half of the fifteenth century and attributed to Niccolò da Verona. In the *Sala delle Figurazioni Sacre* is a *Deposition* from the workshop of Rubens, a *Resurrected Christ* by Lorenzo Lotto (1480-1555) and a *Christ with the Cross* perhaps by Sodoma (Giovan Antonio Bazzi, 1477-1549) or by Giovanfrancesco de' Maineri. In the following *Sala di Alessandro Magno* are seven large paintings by the

articulated by flattened pilaster strips also of the giant order (the bases of the pilasters, too, are articulated with Palladian forms). The rusticated portal leads to the magnificent Neoclassical *Staircase* and, at the top, the *Salone degli Antenati* (with its sixty portraits of members of the family) where two cases contain pottery from the sixteenth to the eighteenth century and weapons. Next come the rooms of the *Picture Gallery*,

greatest Mantuan painter of the eighteenth century, Giuseppe Bazzani (1690-1769), with the deeds of the Alexander the Great. The Neoclassic exedra built in the eighteenth century in the palace courtyard leads to the two Renaissance buildings bought by the d'Arco family in 1872, one originally part of a larger fifteenth-century building. On the ground floor is the Chapel of the d'Arco counts, and on the upper floor

Left: Portrait *of the last Duke of Mantua, attributed to F. Geffels (1707).*

Right and below: *frescoes in the Room of the Zodiac, by Giovan Maria Falconetto (1520).*

is the interesting Sala dello Zodiaco frescoed in 1520 by Giovan Maria Falconetto (1458-1534) with a series of zodiac figures set into a loggia, with glimpses of landscapes and figures seen through the arches (as Mantegna had done in the Camera degli Sposi). Of great interest are the *Constellations*, represented in twelve compartments, with their relative myths. These reveal the attention Falconetto paid to antiquarian culture. His studies also led him to depict a series of classic buildings including the Arena and the Lion Gate of Verona, the Mausoleum of Theodoric

and San Vitale in Ravenna, the Arch of Augustus in Fano and the Colosseum and the Arch of Janus in Rome. Unfortunately the fireplace set against a wall in the seventeenth century replaced one of the painted panels.

(Via 25 Aprile - Via Porto)
CHURCH OF SANTI GERVASIO and PROTASIO

The church, which goes back to the twelfth century, was completely rebuilt in the early nineteenth century by Giovan Battista Vergani (1788-after 1841) who added the present charming facade in 1836. The tall engaged columns below and the three-light window on an axis in the center are manifestly Neoclassic in their inspiration and constitute a clear example in Mantua of the Classicism of the Restoration, part and parcel of the garden in the adjacent Palazzo Cavriani by the same architect.

(Via Trento - Via Cavriani)
PALAZZO CAVRIANI and GARDEN

The palace of the noble Cavriani family was built in 1756 by the Bolognese architect Alfonso Torregiani, on the basis of a rigid formal scheme based on a clear differentiation of the floors with a barely projecting marble portal at the center of the facade. This concept had been brought to Mantua from Bologna where it was inside the houses of nobles and senators that the majestic staircases and luxuriously furnished rooms were given free reign in the accepted fashion of the nobility of the second center of the State of the Church.

The Mantua palace of the Cavriani exemplifies this idea and the majestic monumental staircase and a series of frescoed rooms furnished with exceptional pieces of furniture and paintings counterbalance the austere facade. Across from the palazzo is the Neoclassic garden planned for the Cavriani by Giovan Battista Vergani, the greatest representative of

Church of Santi Gervasio and Protasio (1836).

Restoration Classicism in Mantua. Once more the attention paid to models of Antiquity, of primary importance for those Neoclassic architects who closely adhered to philological studies, predominates, particularly in the articulation of the monumental enclosure, with piers with busts of famous Mantuans at the top of piers, treated like classic herms. At the center of the garden is a statue of *Virgil* by Stefano Girola, who also did the busts.

(Piazza San Leonardo)
CHURCH OF SAN LEONARDO

In the midst of this labyrinth of lanes in the old quarter stands the church of San Leonardo dating, like the nearby church of Santi Gervasio and Protasio, to the thirteenth century. It was completely rebuilt in 1793 (remains of a Romanesque wall with arcading can be seen on the left flank, after the campanile). The classic elements on the austere facade were filtered through a Neoclassic sensitivity which had come to Mantua, via the circles of the Accademia di Belle Arti, from the nearby centers of Milan, Verona and Parma. Inside, about halfway back, is the fifteenth-century

Chapel of San Gottardo, with a sixteenth-century fresco by Lorenzo Costa the Elder of the *Saviour and Prophets* over the altar. Traces of sixteenth-century frescoes are also to be seen in the church, before the sanctuary. A sixteenth-century panel with the *Madonna and Saints* by Francia (1460-1517) stands on the high altar, a demonstration that in the time of Mantegna, Giulio Romano and then Bertani, the building was an important center of worship.

137

(Via Zambelli)

Piazza Virgiliana

The Piazza is the result of reclamation, in 1735, of an area near the Lago di Mezzo which had for centuries been subject to swamping. The idea of turning the large open area into a square however dates to (1835-1925). The figures at the sides are by Giuseppe Menozzi. An amphitheater built in front of the Lago in 1820 was dismantled to make way for this installation.

1797 when Paolo Pozzo, the most important representative of Neoclassicism in Mantua, designed the project when General Miollis, named as governor of Mantua by Napoleon, decided to endow the city with a monumental, classic forum.

This new space was "typical" of Napoleonic cities, and is exemplified by the project for the Foro Bonaparte in nearby Milan, by Giovan Antonio Antolini, dating to 1801.

In addition to building various palaces (such as the one housing the Museo Francesco Gonzaga by Pozzo or the one at no. 17 by Giovan Battista Vergani) the principal objective was to turn the central area of the square into a park with hedges, small columns, rows of trees and marble benches. Another example exists in Padua, in the central part of the island of Prato della Valle (1755). In Mantua, however, the composition was centered around a statue of *Virgil*.

The one there now is by Luca Beltrami (1854-1933), and was cast in bronze by Emilio Quadrelli

Piazza Virgiliana; below: interior of the Museo Diocesano.

138

MUSEO FRANCESCO GONZAGA or MUSEO DIOCESANO

Left: Madonna and Child, *(14th cent.).*

Above: *interior of the Museo Diocesano.*

Below: *Missal of B. of Brandenburg.* Left: Pentecost; right: Crucifixion.

The old Convent of Sant'Agnese was rebuilt in 1795 by Paolo Pozzo who also designed the elegant facade. It was restored after being damaged in World War II (very little remains of the medieval complex) and turned into the Museo Diocesano di Arte Sacra. Various art objects of particular interest are to be noted in the large entrance Hall. In particular, two ivory boxes (nn. 6-7) of Arab-Sicilian workmanship dating to the twelfth-thirteenth century, originally set one inside the other and meant for the ashes of San Celestino. A relief of the *Madonna and Child* (n. 9) of the late fourteenth century, in partially painted gilded silver, is a rare example of French Gothic goldwork. An elegant late Gothic marble statue of *Saint George and the Dragon* (n. 14) also comes from the Cathedral of Mantua. It dates to the very beginning of the fifteenth century and is attributed to Pier Paolo Dalle Masegne who, together with his brother Iacobello, did the Gothic facade of the Cathedral. Two carved wooden panels (nn. 16-17), of a series of six, are an interesting example of the decoration planned for the inside of Alberti's church of San Sebastiano. The central figures (Saint Sebastian and a *Doctor of the Church*) date to the fifteenth century, while the surrounding figures date to the early sixteenth century. A lovely illuminated codex, a *Missal* (n. 18) which belonged to the Marchesa Barbara of Brandenburg, is on exhibit in the hall. It dates to the late fifteenth century and the illuminations are attributed to Belbello di Pavia and Gerolamo da Cremona. The parchment codex of the *Gradual* (n. 19) dates to 1460. Of note among the paintings are the *Ascension of Christ*, a synopia of around 1488, attributed by some to Andrea

Mantegna (but not by Longhi), a *Deposition* from the early sixteenth century, painted on plaster, attributed to Correggio, and a tempera panel with the *Madonna and Child*, attributed to the school of Lorenzo Costa the Elder and also known as the *Madonna of the Apple* (the fruit in the foreground), dating to the early sixteenth century. Lastly a *Crucifixion*, perhaps of the school of Ferrara, oil on canvas, sixteenth century. Among the most precious of the devotional objects is an urn (n. 40) in ebony, quartz and gilded silver, dating to the late sixteenth century and from the basilica of Santa Barbara, used as a reliquary for the Most Precious Blood (in part conserved in the church of Sant'Andrea), made in Venice for Duke Vincenzo I. Another important reliquary urn is the one for the Holy Cross (n. 55), said to contain fragments of the Cross, and made in Byzantium around the tenth century, part of the family treasure of the Paleologhi fam-

ily and brought to Mantua as part of her dowry by Margherita, wife of Guglielmo Gonzaga. Of interest too is a bronze (n. 67) *Crucifixion*, made in 1621 by Pietro Tacca, sculptor at the Medici court, as well as the scene of the *Pace con Pietà*, a relief in gilded silver with enamels, coral and mother of pearl, set in an architectural frame which recalls the facade of the church of Sant'Andrea. After a small section with seven paintings by Giuseppe Bazzani, comes the Arms and Armor section with important examples of Renaissance suits of armor by armorers from Milan and Brescia.

(Via Cairoli)
PALAZZO DEL SEMINARIO

In 1825 Giovan Battista Vergani gave this building, just a few meters from the Cathedral, its Neoclassic facade with symmetrical temple fronts.

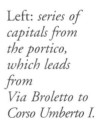

Above: *view of Piazza Marconi (porticoes).*

Left: *series of capitals from the portico, which leads from Via Broletto to Corso Umberto I.*

SURROUNDINGS

- Citadel and Porta Giulia
  (Sant'Antonio)
- Cartiera Burgo (Burgo Paper Mill)
  (Sant'Antonio)
- La Favorita (Porto Mantovano)
- Corte Spinosa (Porto Mantovano)
- Bosco Fontana (Marmirolo)
- Sanctuary of S.M. delle Grazie
  (Curtatone-Le Grazie)
- Sabbioneta
- Abbey of San Polirone
  (S.Benedetto Po)

Porta Giulia, facade (16th cent.) Porta Giulia, traditionally attributed to a design by Giulio Romano, may more likely be by Bertani, since the drawing by Giulio in question is related to an urban gate that was to be built near the Palazzo Te.

CITADEL and PORTA GIULIA
(Citadel, along the Mantua-Verona highway)

The bridge-dam known as dei Mulini which separates the Lago Superiore from the Lago di Mezzo, was initially laid out in 1190 by Alberto Pitentino and leads to the old Citadel. The name comes from the fact that before it was destroyed by the allied bombings of 1944, this passageway was a sort of gallery that consisted of twelve mills or "*mulini*". The present bridge leads to the old Renaissance Citadel, a fortification that defended the city. Practically the only thing left today is the Porta Giulia, built in 1549 to a design by Giulio Romano, according to some, although if later it would have been designed by Bertani. The Citadel was begun in pentagonal form around 1530 as one of the defensive structures. Porta Giulia was not simply a military structure, but was thought of as a real urban entrance for anyone arriving from Verona and Brescia. The only elements for dating are the inscriptions on views which celebrate the wedding of Federico with Margherita Paleologa and the date 1549 regarding restoration. The facades are modelled on a triumphal arch articulated by Doric pilaster strips, as befitted a "fort", with a triangular pediment on the central part. The archway leads to a barrel vaulted rectangular hall, articulated by fine pilaster strips. The general idea was based on that of an ancient bath hall screened by triumphal arches and decorated with stuccowork and reliefs in antique style.

CARTIERA BURGO
(Burgo Paper Mill)
(Citadel, along the Mantua-Verona route)

Between 1960 and 1963 Pier Luigi Nervi and Gino Covre built this marvelous example of an architectural solution to the complex problem of creating a single space to house multiple manufacturing phases, unhampered by supports or dividing walls and employing the same structural system throughout. Pier Luigi Nervi, specialized in designing large structures in reinforced concrete, adopted the static principles employed in constructing suspension bridges (to which the paper mill can visually be assimilated), creating a covering suspended on four coupled pylons located at the ends. The result was completely unlike normal factory buildings, and not only brilliantly resolved a difficult functional problem, but also created a qualifying landmark in the landscape of the surrounding plain. Those who pass by on the highway may find it hard to interpret this structure, for what looks like a passageway (a bridge) is actually a factory.

143

Above:
*architectural
complex of the
Burgo
Paperworks*

*(P.L.Nervi and
G. Covre 1960-
63).*
Below: *Villa la
Favorita*

*(in an eigh-
teenth-century
print).*

When the Duke died, the Favorita was repeatedly looted and was partially torn down in the nineteenth century. After a fire in 1913, it was definitively abandoned. Today the ruins are still a haunting example of the grandeur of the Gonzaga structures and the pomp of their court.

All that is left though is the central structure with two fine loggias. No trace remains of the woods and gardens which originally surrounded it.

LA FAVORITA
(Porto Mantovano, along the Mantua-Verona route)

The villa was built between 1613 and 1624 for Duke Ferdinando by the architect Niccolò Sebregondi and soon became one of the most magnificent Gonzaga residences outside the city. But this building was not only the gilded retreat of the court in specific times of year, for by coupling the requirements of official entertainment with those of a real villa, it was also an example of the colonization and exploitation of agricultural terrain.

CORTE SPINOSA
(Porto Mantovano, along the Mantua-Brescia route)

The Villa di Corte Spinosa is an outstanding six-teenth-century example of how the Gonzagas suc-ceeded in combining the need for a formal qualifica-tion of their domain outside the city, with the requirements of the productive exploitation of agri-cultural lands by means of villas (Corti, for example) which were properly equipped for the storage of agri-cultural produce and with annexes in which to shelter

Above: *Villa la Favorita, facade*

Left: *detail of Corte Spinosa.*

the materials and the workers. The distinctive architectural features employed here suggest that it might have been designed by Giulio Romano, both because of the porticoes articulated in a syntax that is both classicist and rustic, and because of the granary and the pier.

BOSCO FONTANA
(Marmirolo, along the Mantua-Brescia route)

At the end of the sixteenth century Vincenzo Gonzaga had a Hunting Lodge built near a spring which gave its name to the entire zone on the family estate (now a natural reserve, for it is one of the few surviving examples of forest in the entire Plain of the Po). Viani, the architect who oversaw the building of this complex, drew inspiration from various sources. The four towers set at the corners of the square core of the building are clearly of neo-medieval style, while citations from Giulio Romano's Palazzo Te are to be found in the sham pseudo-rustication or, above, in the three arched loggia topped by a triangular pediment.

SANCTUARY OF SANTA MARIA DELLE GRAZIE
(Curtatone-Le Grazie, along the Mantua-Cremona route)

The complex, located about seven kilometers from Mantua in the direction of Cremona, was built between 1399 and 1406 for Francesco I Gonzaga, perhaps by the architect Bartolino da Novara, in thanks for the end of the plague. The simple church facade is preceded by a portico with thirteen round-headed arches and lunettes which were frescoed in the sixteenth century. At the center is a fine portal with a *Madonna and Child* in the style of Mantegna painted in the lunette. The nine chapels inside are particularly interesting. The first one belonged to the Castiglione family. On the back wall is the *Mausoleum of Baldassarre Castiglione*, designed by Giulio Romano, while the frescoes on the vault are by Giulio. There are traces of painting by Lorenzo Costa the Younger in the second chapel, while in the third is an altarpiece with panels painted by Antonio Maria and Giovan Battista Viani in the early seventeenth

Bosco Fontana: view of the complex of the *Palazzina di Caccia (Hunting* *Lodge) (16th cent.).*

Sanctuary of Santa Maria delle Grazie. Above: facade. Left: view of the complex from the lakes or the canebrakes.

century. Every year in August the square is the stage for an exhibition of "street painting" by the so-called *"Madonnari"*.

SABBIONETA

The town of Sabbioneta is one of the most interesting examples of a Renaissance center founded *ex novo* in line with the sixteenth-century architectural dictates, which aimed at creating a rational space distinguished by its order, harmony, perfection and functionality, features which had been the subject of debate for centuries. Since Sabbioneta was created in

Sabbioneta.
Preceding
page: *principal
facade of the
Ducal Palace.*

Sabbioneta.
Above: *Ducal
Palace: in the
background, the
Palace and on*

*the right, detail
of the Church of
Santa Maria
Assunta.*

a milieu of this sort, it is frequently identified as one of the most successful examples of the Renaissance concept of "Ideal City", in other words perfect.

Seat of an autonomous Duchy, of a Gonzaga branch which had no intention of submitting to the Mantua family branch, Sabbioneta was begun in 1564 by Vespasiano Gonzaga as a spacious fortress rather than as a real city (since his State was not that large or extensive). It is not however only an example of military installation like so many others built in Europe, but a real Capital, in which the quality of the buildings was equal, if not superior, to that of the urban layout. Vespasiano, who had been to Spain in the service of Philip II of Spain as governor and military engineer, gave Sabbioneta a hexagonal plan, with projecting star-shaped bastions and the streets laid out in checkerboard fashion. Only the main street or Corso (now Via Vespasiano Gonzaga) seems to have an anomalous layout in this perfect structure, for it does not lead directly to the city gates but has two 90° angles which would have hindered enemy troops attempting to reach the inner core of the city. From the point of view of architecture, the orthogonal network of streets and blocks, closer together in the eastern area, served as a basic ground plan into which the palaces, churches and houses, whose aspect was not at all military, could be fitted. The individual buildings are often outstanding examples of architecture. In

1564 work on these buildings was begun by a series of "masters", whose names remain unknown, with the exception of the architect Vincenzo Scamozzi. Vespasiano Gonzaga, with his military experience, planned the military layout of the center. It is highly probable that the buildings were designed by various architects. The main structure is the residence of the dukes of Sabbioneta, the *Palazzo Ducale*, or "Palazzo Grande", built between 1568 and 1577. The facade on the square has a loggia with five rusticated arches on the ground floor. The interior is frescoed and subdivided into various rooms with rich wooden ceilings, busts and statues of the Sabbioneta Gonzagas.

At one side of the square is the *Church of Santa Maria Assunta* (1580-1592), with a single nave and side chapels. The eighteenth-century frescoes by Giorgio Anselmi are interesting, while the dome over the fifth Chapel on the right (of the Sacred Heart), with openwork against a blue ground and scenographically quite effective, was done in 1768 by Antonio Galli Bibiena, who had also designed the

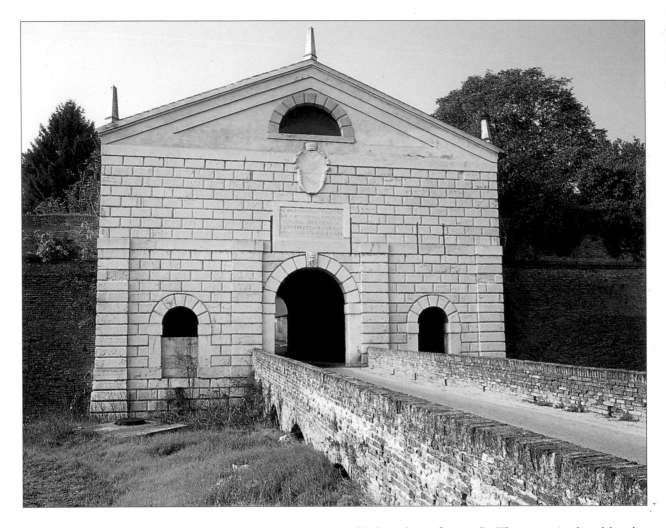

Sabbioneta,   *Imperiale*
Porta Urbica,   *(1579).*
known as

Pavilion of the Kaffeehaus in the Ducal Palace in Mantua, similar in style. Nearby is the octagonal Church of the *Incoronata*, which Vespasiano had built between 1586 and 1588 to house his mausoleum (realized in 1592 by Gian Battista della Porta).

Of particular note in the city is the *Teatro Olimpico*, designed in 1588 by Vincenzo Scamozzi, who finished works by Palladio (in particular the Teatro Olimpico of Vicenza) and Sansovino. The rectangular interior has wooden tiers and a columned upper loggia as prescribed for classic theaters by the Latin author Vitruvius in his treatise on architecture. The frescoes on the walls are of the Venetian School and date to the sixteenth century.

An honorary column (with a statue, in this case *Pallas Athena*, on top) dating to 1584 stands at the center of Piazza Castello or d'Armi. *The Palazzo del Giardino* was built between 1577 and 1588 as Vespasiano's private residence (the facade may origi-

nally have been frescoed). The space is closed by the unique *Galleria degli Antichi*, initially known as the "Corridor Grande", built in 1583-84 to house the Duke's collections of antiquities. This may be the only wing that corresponds to an antique square or forum as described by Alberti (whose treatise was thoroughly studied in the late sixteenth century), surrounded by porticoes devoid of architectural orders since they were to serve as galleries from which to watch gladiatorial spectacles. The gallery, which runs along for almost one hundred meters and is raised on twenty-six arches, was originally probably plastered and painted.

The large cornice molding at the top is the result of restoration. Sculptured reliefs (if possible antique like the statues inside) or inscriptions were surely to have been set into the empty panels on the end walls and on the pilasters framing the windows, always the case in buildings of antique cast (such as Alberti's Tempio Malatestiano in Rimini), just as the empty niches, hollowed out below the panels in the piers, would also have contained statues. It must have been quite magnificent then, not nearly as austere as it

Sabbioneta.
Above: *Galleria degli Antenati (Gallery of Ancestors).*
Left: *detail of the bays (1583-84).*

Pages 152-153: *Teatro Olimpico or all'Antica (interior, 1588-90).*

appears today. It was modeled on descriptions in ancient sources of rooms to be used as a Museum, which Giulio Romano and Bertani had in part also reproposed on the inner walls of the *Galleria dei Marmi* in the Palazzo Ducale in Mantua, and which could be designed only by an architect who was well versed in antique studies.

Above:
Sabbioneta,
Cloister of the
Incoronata
(1586-88).

ABBEY OF SAN POLIRONE
(San Benedetto Po)

In 1007 the Benedictines founded the abbey of Polirone near the Po river. It was enlarged by Matilda of Canossa, passed to the Cistercians and eventually became one of the favorite sanctuaries of the Gonzaga, who infused it with new life in 1420 by joining it to the Chapter of the Reformed Congregation of Santa Giustina in Padua. Between 1537 and 1546 Giulio Romano put into effect a series of substantial renovations for the Gonzaga. In

1797 Napoleon suppressed the congregation and the abbey buildings were torn down and abandoned. They were later radically restored. The facade of the church has a portico with loggia inspired by Giulio Romano, with an eighteenth-century addition above. The structure and decoration of the interior are also in line with Giulio Romano's renovations: the coffered ceiling of the nave and the dome, and the classicist Serlian openings which separate the nave from the two side-aisles. The fresco decorations in the ten chapels on the side-aisles are by the school of Giulio Romano. The *tomb of the Countess Matilda of Canossa* is in the Sacristy, although her body was taken to Rome in the eighteenth century.

The Romanesque church of *Santa Maria*, with a fine mosaic floor of 1151, is also part of the complex, while the fresco by Correggio in the *Refectory* dates to 1513-14.

Abbey of Polirone.
Right, top to bottom: *the cloisters;* below: *the facade.*

Cittadella

Corte
S. Giovanni Bono

Lago Inf

Lago di Mezzo

Lago Superiore

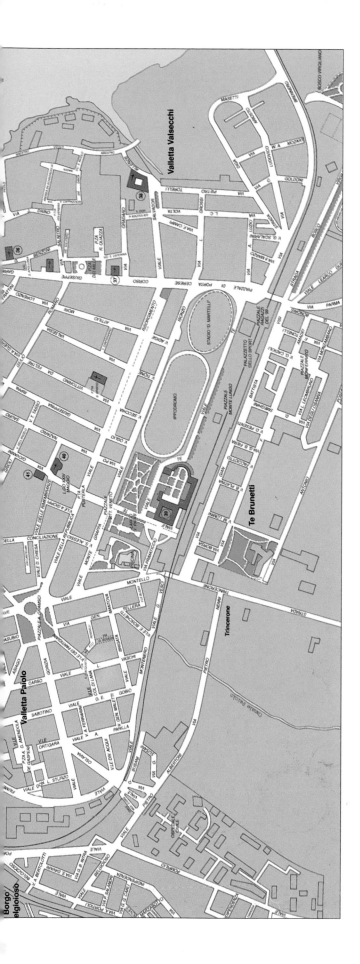

KEY

1. Church of S. Leonardo
2. Monument to Virgil
3. Museo Diocesano
4. Palazzo Vescovile
5. Palazzo Bonacolsi
6. Duomo (Cathedral)
7. Rigoletto's House
8. Ducal Palace
9. Castle of S.Giorgio
10. Church of S. Barbara
11. Museo del Risorgimento
12. Palazzo del Podestà or del Broletto
13. Museo Tazio Nuvolari
14. Palazzo della Ragione
15. Clock Tower
16. Rotonda of S. Lorenzo
17. Teatro Scientifico
18. State Archives
19. Town Library
20. Basilica of S. Andrea
21. Town Hall
22. Teatro Sociale
23. Church of S. Orsola
24. Palazzo d'Arco
25. Church of S. Francesco
26. Railroad Station
27. Church of S. Maurizio
28. House of Giulio Romano
29. Church of S. Barnaba
30. Palazzo di Giustizia
31. Prefecture
32. Tower of S. Domenico
33. Fifteenth-century palazzo
34. Palazzo Valenti
35. Andreasi House
36. Church of S. Apollonia
37. Church of S. Caterina
38. Church of S. Maria del Gradaro
39. Palazzo Te
40. Church of S. Sebastiano
41. Mantegna's House
42. Post Office
43. Arrivabene Tower
44. Belfiore Memorial
45. Monument to Andreas Hoeffler

SUGGESTED BIBLIOGRAPHY

C.Cunaccia, M.Listri, R.Signorini, *Rivedere Mantova*, Florence, 1996
Leon Battista Alberti, Catalog of the Exhibition edited by J.Rykwert and A.Engel, Milan, 1994

R.Berzaghi, *Il Palazzo Ducale di Mantova*, Milan, 1992

G.Bombi, *Mantova*, Milan, 1992

C.Berselli, *La Storia di Mantova. Compendio*, Mantua, 1991

Giulio Romano, *Catalog of the Exhibition*, Milan, 1989

E.Marani, *Guida di Mantova*, Mantua, 1987

S.Bertelli, *The Courts of the Italian Renaissance*, New York, 1986